FUELED BY FAITH

Books by Jennifer Kennedy Dean
from New Hope Publishers

Legacy of Prayer
Live a Praying Life
Riches Stored in Secret Places
The Life-Changing Power in the Blood of Christ
The Life-Changing Power in the Name of Jesus

FUELED
by FAITH

Living Vibrantly in the POWER OF PRAYER

JENNIFER KENNEDY DEAN

new
hope
PUBLISHERS

Birmingham, Alabama

New Hope® Publishers
P. O. Box 12065
Birmingham, AL 35202-2065

All Scripture quotations, unless otherwise indicated, are taken from the HOLY BIBLE, NEW INTERNATIONAL VERSION®. NIV®. Copyright ©1973, 1978, 1984 by International Bible Society. Used by permission of Zondervan. All rights reserved.

Scripture quotations marked (NASB) are taken from the New American Standard Bible®, Copyright © 1960, 1962, 1963, 1968, 1971, 1972, 1973, 1975, 1977, 1995 by The Lockman Foundation. Used by permission.

Scripture quotations marked (KJV) are taken from The Holy Bible, King James Version.

ISBN: 1-56309-993-4

Dedication

To my husband, Wayne,
and to our sons,
Brantley, Kennedy, and Stinson

But the plans of the LORD stand firm forever,
the purposes of his heart through all generations.
—Psalm 33:11

Acknowledgments

Thank you, Terry Trieu, for your years of selfless ministry to me as you did the heavy lifting, both literally and figuratively, while I pursued my call. I'll never find another assistant like you.

Thank you, Mary Medley, Wanda Kanai, Joanne Stokes, and Mary Lee Butler, for your intercession. You bear my burdens as if they were your own—faithful friends.

Thank you, Dr. Dan DeMarque—little nephew all grown up—for the use of your wonderful mountain house where I retreated to do final edits on this book.

Thank you, Mom and Dad, for showing me how life looks when faith fuels it.

Table of Contents

Introduction

Life in the kingdom of God is fueled by faith. "The righteous will live by faith" (Romans 1:17). The exercise of faith brings all the promises of God into the atmosphere of earth. "The promise comes by faith" (Romans 4:16).

Faith is the force that fuels every action in the kingdom. To learn the ways of faith is to discover the keys to the kingdom. The kingdom of God is the dimension of reality in which you can live right now. You can have all the riches of the kingdom, all the authority of the kingdom, all the power of the kingdom as your present-tense experience. You can escape the fear and futility that fuels your flesh and live instead in the fullness of the promises of God.

Faith suits you to operate in the kingdom's atmosphere. Just as your physical body is fitted and designed to thrive in earth's atmosphere, so your spiritual nature is suited to the stratosphere of the heavenly realms.

I invite you to join me in this journey of faith. I'm convinced that the more we understand about how faith operates, the more strategically we will use it. The Bible is the faith textbook. God breathed much into His Word that explains faith, dissects faith, and teaches what faith is made of and how faith operates. Since that is so, it must be important for us to understand faith so that we can experience its fullness.

We'll examine faith as follows:

Faith: The Focus

Have faith in God, not in an outcome. God Himself is the focus of faith. To understand faith, we have to know the Faith Giver.

Faith: The Foundation

Faith is built on the living word of God—the word that He is now speaking into your life. The same word that framed the world is now framing your world. Faith is not believing *something*. Faith is believing *Someone*.

Faith: The Function

To operate fully in the power of faith, we have to understand how faith works. How do we live minute-by-minute in the full-throttle power of God? God has invited us to live right now in the kingdom, fueled by faith.

Faith: The Finish

Faith, in its finished form, brings all the power of God into the circumstances of earth. God puts the finishing touches on our faith by allowing and engineering circumstances that bring us face-to-face with the residual flesh still operating in our lives where faith could operate instead. When we understand how God is circumcising our faith—cutting all the flesh away—we will be able to cooperate fully with His processes.

Abandoned to Him

At the age of 20, I made an unreserved commitment of my life to Jesus Christ. I had made a genuine profession of faith many years before that, but I reached a juncture at which I had to decide the trajectory of my life. Would I be satisfied to follow the rules of my religion and mouth its doctrines correctly? Would I act out the roles cast for me by culture and tradition, sometimes masquerading as righteousness? Or would I respond to this nagging sense of dissatisfaction that hinted at the possibility of something more? A steady drumbeat deep inside seemed to lure me to another path. I was being wooed by the Spirit's invitation: "Why do you seek the living among the dead?" And I could not resist Him.

During the 30-plus years that have followed, I have passionately pursued a present-tense relationship with the living and indwelling Jesus. I have narrowed my goals to one goal for every moment that I live: to be completely and utterly abandoned to Him. I don't know where that will lead me, but wherever it leads me, that is where I'm going. People often ask me, "What is your five-year plan?" My answer: "To be completely and utterly abandoned to Him." Long ago I learned that following the Ruler instead of the rules would take me down paths I could not have imagined. Every day I traverse new terrain, desperately dependent upon the moment-by-moment guidance of Jesus because He is leading me into new territory. He reminds me that my eyes must be fastened on Him; "then you will know which way to go, since you have never been this way before" (Joshua 3:4).

Let me assure you that I have not abandoned sound doctrine. I have no desire to live my life guided by anything but truth. The danger I want to avoid is twofold. First, I don't want to impose pre-packaged beliefs handed down to me by human beings upon the pure truth of the living, active Word of the living, active God. Second, I don't want to depend on and put my faith in my ability to follow a set of religious rules that appear godly on the exterior, but are stuffed with flesh-based motivations. Do you realize that Jesus' detractors were the most religious men of the day? The men who most scrupulously followed all the laws and propounded only the most accepted theological thought? They were so carefully following the letter of the law that they missed the Spirit of the Law embodied in Jesus. They looked right into His face and did not see Him. His words fell upon their ears, but they did not hear Him. I recoil at such a possibility. My heart cries, "Show me your face, let me hear your voice; for your voice is sweet, and your face is lovely" (Song of Songs 2:14).

I want to show you what I am learning about rock-solid truth and sound doctrine as I am learning to live out a life fueled by faith. From the days when I took my first tentative baby steps, tripped and fell and tried again, until my steps became steadier as I navigated the kingdom landscape, I have lived all these years in a faith lab. Every day I put faith to the test, and every day my walk becomes more confident and sure. I still trip and fall and get up and try again. Certainly I have much left to learn. If you are following a set of beliefs, you can finally learn them all. If you are following the Master, there is no end to the learning.

As your journey takes you deeper into the kingdom, you discover that the kingdom's land formations are many and varied. Today is not like yesterday and tomorrow will not be like today—if you keep moving.

In the kingdom landscape you will find mountains and valleys one day, fertile river land lush with foliage another. Still another day will bring you to quiet green pastures laced with gentle streams of still water. Keep moving and you may find yourself walking a well-traveled, brightly-lit path, but the next day might find you on a path so untravelled and dark you feel like a blind person feeling your way step by step. One path may lead you to the banks of a river so full it is overflowing its banks. Another path on another day will take you into a desert that seems desolate and bare. But it is all the kingdom. If you plan to search out the kingdom's treasures, you will have to learn its landscape.

A faith walk will bring you into the adventure of a strange dichotomy of work and rest, not interchangeably, but simultaneously. You are acting—working—from a foundation of rest. So your work, your effort, is an expression of your soul's restful state. If that makes no sense to you right now, it will by the time you finish this book.

Faith is not passive. It is active and aggressive and—if I dare say it—greedy. Faith wants it all! God gives, faith takes. What is the "all" that greedy faith demands? Nothing less than everything God has to give. Paul defined "all" in one word: Jesus. "But Christ is all, and is in all" (Colossians 3:11). A faith walk is living every moment in absolute dependence on the living, indwelling Christ, knowing that the more you die to your flesh, the more of Him you will experience. One taste of *His life through you* instead of *your life for Him*, and you will be caught forever. In a faith walk, you shed flesh as you go. You molt. Every step deeper leaves the limitations of flesh behind, abandoned, and reveals the life of Christ.

This book is not designed to be a passive read. I will invite you to handle the Word of God for yourself as you go. I will challenge you to let the Spirit think His thoughts in you. You will find the book sprinkled with interactive questions. These questions are not designed to test your knowledge, but to allow you to "examine the Scriptures daily to find out whether these things [are] so" (Acts 17:11 NASB). The questions will cause you to examine your life in the light of His Word and discover how to move from following the rules to following the Ruler. The point of a faith walk is that it is not academic and sterile, but it is daily and gritty and raucous. And fun. So I want you to dive in, not just tiptoe around the edges.

Leave behind tame, timid, play-it-safe, follow-the-rules faith. Learn to exercise an outrageous, get-out-of-the-boat, resurrection faith.

❧

<u>*Section One*</u>

FAITH:
The Focus

❧

Chapter One

ENOUGH FAITH

I tell you the truth, if you have faith as small as a mustard seed, you can say to this mountain, "Move from here to there" and it will move. Nothing will be impossible for you.

—Matthew 17:20

D o you have enough faith? If you are like most Christians, your answer is no. Maybe you say it with shame, feeling that if you were more spiritual or a better Christian, you would have "enough faith." Maybe you say it piously, thinking that no one could possibly have "enough faith." Maybe you think it would be unseemly and arrogant to answer yes.

Don't edit yourself or try to figure out the right answer. There is no right answer. Just respond honestly. Do you have enough faith? Why did you answer as you did? What experiences or beliefs have convinced you that you either do or do not have enough faith?

I'm going to make some guesses. I'm going to guess that many of you answered no to the question, "Do you have enough faith?" Somewhere along the line, your faith has taken a hit from which you have not recovered. Maybe you explained it something like this: "I had faith that God would heal my son, but he died. I must not have had enough faith." Or maybe your story goes like this: "I had faith that God would restore my marriage, but my husband went through with the divorce. I feel that God let me down. Now I can't make myself believe that I can trust God for anything." My own journey to understand prayer and the faith that lays prayer's foundation began with just such an experience.

My Faith Passage

The summer following my graduation from high school, my only brother, who was two years my junior and my best friend, was diagnosed with a rare and deadly form of leukemia. Because of my mother's strong prayer network and my parents' absolute faith in God, Roger's illness was covered in prayer continually. We firmly believed that his body would be restored and even when his symptoms worsened that belief did not waver. Throughout the year of his illness, we saw many instances of healing—times when the doctors gave up hope, or when a new and serious symptom would emerge. When he was first diagnosed, the immediate life-threatening danger was a large cantaloupe-sized tumor that was crushing his bronchial tubes, making difficult for him to breathe, and had pushed his organs out of place so that his heart was beside his stomach. It was already at such a stage that Roger's death could be only days away. Our church opened its doors to the community for prayer and word is that a standing-room-only crowd attended. Our family was at the hospital 100 miles away, but many who were present report that there was a discernable, almost physical sense of the Lord's presence. By the next morning, the tumor had shrunk by half. A week later it was gone entirely. Time and time again miraculous healing of symptoms occurred and it affirmed our faith. Yet a year after his disease had been diagnosed, my sweet brother died, the withered shell of his body lying in a hospital bed.

As sick as he was, the news of his death was the last thing I expected to hear. Yet at that moment, what I can only describe as a blanket of peace covered me. My family members all report the same experience. I did not know the Lord and His ways well at that time. But I did not have to do or believe anything to receive His love, which truly overpowered what the responses of my flesh would have been. His intervention in every detail of the situation continued to be obvious as He comforted us in supernatural ways.

Later, left-brain analytical thinker that God has created me to be, I began to wonder, "If all that prayer for my brother's healing was going on, and Roger died anyway, what good was prayer?" This question compelled me into a search for answers and understanding that has defined the call of God on my life. God produced something eternal through Roger's death. His life was a seed that fell into the ground to produce a harvest.

Explaining Away

You will hear many trite and unsatisfying answers to the questions about faith that such an experience births. Someone will be sure to say, "You didn't have enough faith." You might search your memory for moments of uncertainty and doubt and, to your shame, recall just such feelings along the way. Since then, you have been saddled with the terrible burden of feeling that if only you could have had enough faith, things would have turned out differently. You find yourself afraid to exercise faith, knowing that you failed at faith just when your faith was most necessary.

Another explanation you are sure to hear is, "People have free will. God doesn't force anyone. We live in an evil world and sometimes evil wins." If you accept that theory, you develop a theology that says sometimes God chooses to be passive in the face of determined evil. Your understanding of God is that He is free will's victim and sometimes slinks away in defeat. How can you really trust that God? Aren't the outcomes of most circumstances contingent upon some human's decision? So wouldn't God be thwarted more times than not?

Explanations are easy to find. Because Satan, who fathers all lies, is a skilled and practiced liar, his lies sound like the truth. He is no amateur. His lies will seem to be the most logical summation of the facts.

He will present arguments that the evidence appears to support. Let me take this opportunity to preview for you what you are going to discover as you work through this book: appearance is not truth. The evidence upon which we base our understanding is not in the facts we see, but in the truth we know. We examine "the evidence of things not seen" (Hebrews 11:1 KJV). From the Scriptures, we are going to build a careful and precise definition of faith and then examine in great detail how faith works. You may be feeling inadequate or defeated right now, but when you know the truth, the truth will make you free.

Where you are in your understanding of faith right now is not an issue. You are at your starting place. It is no accident that this book is in your hands and that your eyes are on this page.

Don't be afraid to be honest with God. Listen to what Job said when he felt disillusioned with God: "I will give free reign to my complaint and speak out in the bitterness of my soul" (Job 10:1). God did not condemn Job for his openness, but instead complimented him for speaking what is right (Job 42:7–8). It was Job's honesty with himself before God that opened the way for God to reach him with the truth.

As you begin this journey to understand how to walk fueled by faith, what past experiences with faith are holding you back? Stop now and name them. Commit all these experiences, struggles, and longings to the Father. Don't let them hold you back any longer. Instead, let them propel you forward. Invite God to use these experiences as entry points where He can bring light. Trust Him. He is the one and only guide on your faith walk, and it is His joy and delight to lead you in the ways of faith. "Do not be afraid, little flock, for your Father has been pleased to give you the kingdom" (Luke 12:32).

Refocusing Faith

Let's go back to the experience of the person who says something like, "I had faith that God would do a certain thing, and then He didn't." I will have to challenge you. You did not have *faith*. You had *belief*. You cannot have faith in an *outcome*. You can only have faith in a *person*. Jesus said, "Have faith *in God*."

Many times our attempts to exercise faith are in hopes that we will be able to manipulate circumstances and bring about our preferred outcome by means of faith expressed through prayer, which is spoken faith. Is that true of you, or am I the only one? That's where I began: *If I can learn how faith operates through prayer, then I can get God to do what I think He should do when I think He should do it. If I can understand how faith works, I can get everything to go my way.* Listen to the voice of experience: it doesn't work. This is a path fraught with disappointment. This kind of thinking is not faith. It is a flesh-fueled, fruitless endeavor. It is belief, but it is not faith.

Belief is not faith. You can make yourself believe anything. What you believe does not have to be true. In the terrorist attacks against the United States on September 11, 2001, on flight 92, which crashed outside Pittsburgh, PA, the flight voice recorder records the terrorists screaming "Allah O Akbar!" as they plummeted to their death. In a shootout in Pakistan between alleged terrorists and the police, the news media recently reported, the dying terrorists wrote on the walls in their blood as they died, "Allah O Akbar!" They believed so fervently that they gave their lives. No one could have a stronger belief than did the men I have just described. They believed something—a set of ideas, a theology.

> *You cannot have faith in an outcome. You can only have faith in a person. Jesus said, "Have faith in God."*

Faith is not *believing something*. Faith is *believing Someone*. "And Abraham believed God…" The first layer in the Scripture's definition of faith is this: *faith is obedience to the present-tense voice of God.* We'll elaborate on this in the next chapter. For right now, I want you to be clear on the idea that faith is not marching in lock-step with a set of beliefs. It is not giving intellectual assent to a doctrinal position. Faith is hearing and responding to God.

> "Faith comes from hearing the message, and the message is heard through the word of Christ" (Romans 10:17). Faith comes from hearing the message. Does that mean everyone whose physical ears hear the message receives faith? The whole context of the message in Romans 10 is that not everyone who hears the message with physical ears accepts it. Only in those who hear the message "through the word of Christ" is faith produced. "Word" in this verse is *rhema*—the present voicing of a word; the speaking word. The one who hears with spiritual ears—who hears Christ Himself speaking the message into his heart—finds that the message gives birth to faith. The Living Voice stimulates the faith-organ and causes it to function properly. Faith is your God-given capacity to receive and act on spiritual knowledge. "By faith Abraham…obeyed" (Hebrews 11:8).
>
> —Jennifer Kennedy Dean, *Live a Praying Life*

Is it possible to have belief, but not faith? Read the following passage.

> *When Jesus had finished these parables, he moved on from there. Coming to his hometown, he began teaching the people in their synagogue, and they were amazed. "Where did this man get this wisdom and these miraculous powers?" they asked. "Isn't this the carpenter's son? Isn't his mother's name Mary, and aren't his brothers James, Joseph, Simon and Judas? Aren't all his sisters with us? Where then did this man get all these things?" And they took offense at him. But Jesus said to them, "Only in his hometown and in his own house is a prophet without honor." And he did not do many miracles there because of their lack of faith.*
>
> —Matthew 13:53–58

Did the people in Jesus' hometown believe that He could perform miracles? Notice their first comment about Him. "Where did this man get this wisdom and these miraculous powers?" Did they have belief? Did they believe that He was able to perform miracles? They had *no doubt* that Jesus was able to do miraculous works.

Why did Jesus not do many miracles there? "And he did not do many miracles there because of their lack of faith." Did they have faith? They did not.

You will notice that the people did not disbelieve that He could do miracles. In fact, they were amazed at His miraculous powers. It was not lack of belief about what He could do that is called "their lack of faith." It was their refusal to embrace who He was. They had confidence in His ability to do miracles—they had belief. But they did not have faith. They were not willing to abandon themselves to Him, trusting Him to be all they needed or desired. Throughout this book, we will progressively discover the difference between belief and faith.

This brings us to the second layer of Scripture's definition of faith. *Faith is trusting God, no matter the outcome; faith is coming to Him with your need, no matter how weak your faith may be.* When you turn to Him, even if you are quaking and drowning in doubt, that is all the faith it takes to release all of His power and provision. Just as belief is not the same as faith, so unbelief is not the same as doubt.

We often look to the story of Peter's experience of attempting to walk on water as an example of how faith does not operate. I suggest to you that it is a picture of how faith does operate. Read the story.

> *But Jesus immediately said to them: "Take courage! It is I. Don't be afraid."*
>
> *"Lord, if it's you," Peter replied, "tell me to come to you on the water."*
>
> *"Come," he said.*
>
> *Then Peter got down out of the boat, walked on the water and came toward Jesus. But when he saw the wind, he was afraid and, beginning to sink, cried out, "Lord, save me!"*

Immediately Jesus reached out his hand and caught him. "You of little faith," he said, "why did you doubt?"

And when they climbed into the boat, the wind died down. Then those who were in the boat worshiped him, saying, "Truly you are the Son of God."

—Matthew 14:27–33

I would agree that Peter failed at his attempt to walk on the water. But I think that Peter's failure taught him something about Jesus that would cause him to be able to live fueled by faith. Here is my favorite line in the story: "Immediately Jesus reached out his hand and caught him." I think it is likely that Jesus had an amused smile on His face when He said to Peter, "Peter! You walked on water! Now, if only you had kept your eyes fixed on Me….Remember that key later when I call you to bigger risks than walking on water."

Here is what I think Peter learned that was more valuable to him than his "success" would have been: *I can boldly respond to Jesus' voice because even if I slip, He will not let me drown.* How else would he ever learn that about Jesus? Peter struggled with doubt, but not with unbelief. In a faith lab, you will sometimes learn what works by learning what doesn't work.

Faith's focus is God, not an outcome. When you have enough faith to turn to Him, no matter the state of your feelings, then you have enough faith. Tell Him about your weak and wobbly faith. Only He can remedy it. Trying to chase doubt from your heart is a useless exercise. Just don't let your enemy convince you that you cannot come to the Father until all your doubts have been erased and you can bring Him perfect faith. That is the subtle lie that is the root of the argument, "You didn't have enough faith." Do you see what that reasoning suggests? It means that your faith is your work. If only *you* can come up with enough faith to trade in for God's favors, then you can determine the outcome. Then, when everything turns out as you thought it should, you can take a bow. After all, you had enough faith. But when things take a direction you did not anticipate, then hang your head in shame. You failed. You did not have enough faith.

Faith Is a Gift

Where does faith come from? Did you come up with it? Do you produce it? No. Faith is a gift from God. He *gives* you faith.

Take note of the words or phrases that answer the question: how does the Scripture tell us that we obtained faith?

> *It is Jesus' name and the faith that comes **through him** that has given this complete healing to him, as you can all see.*
>
> —Acts 3:16

> *For by the grace given me I say to every one of you: Do not think of yourself more highly than you ought, but rather think of yourself with sober judgment, in accordance with the measure of faith **God has given you.***
>
> —Romans 12:3

> *For it is by grace you have been saved, through faith—and this not from yourselves, **it is the gift of God.***
>
> —Ephesians 2:8

God has given you faith. He has put faith on deposit in you. Is it possible that He made a mistake and did not give you enough faith? Is it possible that He has accidentally allowed circumstances into your life for which He did not give you enough faith?

"Just as you received Christ Jesus as Lord, continue to live in him" (Colossians 2:6). The word Paul uses for "live" is the Greek word *peripateo*, which means "to walk around." The Hebrew law of *Halachah* means "law of walking." It is the sacred name for practical instruction in the law concerning the daily walk of life. We are to walk around, living the details of our daily lives, with the same kind of faith through which we received Him as Lord—by simply receiving what He offers and responding to His initiative.

Faith operates the same way for living daily as it does for receiving Him as Lord. The primary player in this daily drama of faith-walking is God. Sometimes I am tempted to assign the starring role to "my faith," by which I usually mean my ability to make something happen by believing it. I am tempted to believe that my own effort to maintain a certain feeling will accomplish something. Self-effort, what the Scripture calls "work," is the opposite of faith. In fact, self-effort cancels out faith.

> *Now when a man works, his wages are not credited to him as a gift, but as an obligation. However, to the man who **does not work** but **trusts God** who justifies the wicked, his **faith** is credited as righteousness. David says the same thing when he speaks of the blessedness of the man to whom God credits righteousness **apart from works**.*
>
> —Romans 4:4–6

We are not saved by self-effort and we do not live in the Spirit by self-effort. If I had to summon up "enough faith" each time I called on God, then what would God's blessings depend on? My ability to summon up the proper amount of faith. But God's blessings are free, unearned, undeserved. I cannot buy them with my faith.

Throughout this book, you will learn how to make use of the faith that is yours as a gift from God. You will discover that God has made it clear. He has not hidden or disguised the truth about faith. You will find that a faith walk is sure and steady.

Questions for Discussion

1. How did you respond when I asked you if you had enough faith?

2. Why did you respond as you did?

3. Are you convinced that God has given you faith?

4. Do you have enough faith?

Chapter Two

THE FAITH GIVER

For it is by grace you have been saved, through faith—and this not from yourselves, it is the gift of God—not by works, so that no one can boast.

—Ephesians 2:8–9

Faith is a gift. God gives it to you. It is part of your inheritance when you are born into the kingdom. All kingdom-dwellers have faith. Faith is the spiritual organ that makes you suited to the atmosphere in the kingdom. The righteous live by faith.

In the kingdom of God, faith is our native air. "In him we live and move and have our being" (Acts 17:28). In Him we live and move and exist at our optimum. Have you ever spent time in a location where the air was different from your native air? Your lungs are acclimated to where you live. The air your lungs are accustomed to breathing has a certain mix of oxygen and nitrogen and certain pollens and a certain level of humidity. When you breathe this air, you lungs work most efficiently. If you were to go to another location, say move from a low altitude to a higher altitude, the air has less oxygen. Since it is not your native air, breathing becomes difficult. Your lungs have a harder time getting the right amount of oxygen to your cells, and your energy level decreases. What is natural in your native air is difficult and strained in this alien air. Your body does not work as efficiently. Your productivity is compromised.

Faith is our native air once we are born into the kingdom of God. It is there for the taking. It is the biosphere of the kingdom. It is a gift to you. Faith fuels your walk in the kingdom.

Gift Givers

A gift is the expression of the giver. I have decorated my office with gifts. Everywhere I look in my office, my eye falls on a gift. I see an owl-shaped vase that my son Stinson made me in art camp as a preschooler. It is all lopsided and rough. I only know it is an owl because he told me so. I look at it and I can remember when he presented it to me with such pride, and I can still see the merriment in his eyes when he proclaimed with great flourish, "It holds real water!" I look to my right and my gaze falls on a paperweight that Kennedy made for me in kindergarten. I look at it and I see Kennedy's little face as I unwrapped his Mother's Day gift. How he intently watched my face to see if it lit up at his handiwork. Inscribed on the back in his juvenile handwriting it says, "To the best best mom." Gifts from my husband, from friends, sisters, parents. Every gift reminds me of its giver. Each gift is a reflection of the giver's personality and taste and interests. Each gift says something about my relationship with the giver. Each gift says something about how the giver feels about me.

Faith is a gift from God. This incredible gift from the Father is the title deed that entitles you to access all the riches of the kingdom. Faith is the key that unlocks the kingdom's gates. It is a lavish gift. A gift of stunning generosity and outlandish love. What does that tell us about the Giver?

Loving

First, it tells you how much He loves you. He loves you so much that He makes available to you *all* of His riches. *All*. One more time: *all* of His riches. By the exercise of faith, all of His power and all of His provision are accessible to you. He has no desire to withhold anything from you. "What's Mine is yours," He says to you. "He who did not spare his own Son, but gave him up for us all—how will he not also, along with him, graciously give us all things?" (Romans 8:32).

Consider what He has said to you: *He who did not spare His own Son...*

Paul, a Jewish writer addressing a primarily Jewish audience, uses a phrase that directly references an Old Testament event, an event that was pivotal to the birthing of the Hebrew nation and was central in Jewish history. It was not an obscure story, known only to the learned. Any Jewish person who read Paul's words would immediately hear them as an echo of God's words to Abraham.

In Genesis 22:1–18, God called Abraham and commanded him, "Take your son, your *only son*, Isaac, whom you love, and go to the region of Moriah. Sacrifice him there as a burnt offering on one of the mountains I will tell you about" (Genesis 22:2). To encapsulate the story, Abraham obeyed God, took his son Isaac to the appointed spot, tied him to the altar, and lifted up his hand to plunge the knife into Isaac and offer him as a sacrifice in obedience to God's voice. At this moment—had his hand already begun its downward arc?—the voice of God came again to Abraham. "'Do not lay a hand on the boy,' he said. 'Do not do anything to him. Now I know that you fear God, because you have not withheld from me your son, your only son'" (Genesis 22:12). (We will revisit this account several times as we discover the principles of faith, because this is the event that the New Testament points to over and over again as the demonstration of what faith means. We will mine truth from its details and burrow into its layers. Keep it bookmarked in your Bible.)

God had required of Abraham his very heart and soul. Do you think Abraham owned anything—even his own life—that he would not have given gladly in place of his son, his only son, Isaac, whom he loved? Once Abraham's willingness to give God his only son had been put on display for the ages, was there any question that everything Abraham owned was God's for the asking? Paul draws upon this account, brings it over into the present moment, and says, "He who did not spare his own Son, but gave him up for us all—how will he not also, along with him, graciously give us all things?" (Romans 8:32).

Paul points us to another Father, another Son. Watch as the Father places the wood for the altar on the Son's back and watches Him walk up the mountain toward the place of the offering. Look into the Father's heart as He relinquishes His Son, His only Son, whom He loves, as He watches His beloved Son in whom He is well-pleased stagger under the weight of the sins piled on His back while He marches toward His violent, cruel, savage death.

This time there is no stay of execution. This time the blood flows. This time the sacrifice is fully carried out. And the nails that pierce the hands of the Son pierce the heart of the Father.

"This is how God showed his love among us: He sent his one and only Son into the world that we might live through him. This is love: not that we loved God, but that he loved us and sent his Son as an atoning sacrifice for our sins" (1 John 4:9–10). Is there anything left for Him to prove?

The Hebrew word used in Genesis 22, translated "withhold," is the word *chasak*. The word means "to hold back for your own personal use" or "to keep in reserve." The word shares a primary Hebrew letter with the word usually translated "holy" (*qadash*), which means "to be completely set apart, to be consecrated for a specific use." Their common letter is the Hebrew letter

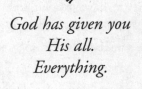

God has given you His all. Everything.

shin. *Shin* stands for wholeness or completeness and always suggests some element of that thought in the words containing it. *Shin*, as you see, pictures three elements brought together to complete one unit, making the *shin* whole or complete. So Abraham did not set Isaac aside to keep him completely and wholly for himself. He did not keep Isaac in his two-fisted grasp and say, "Mine! *All* mine!" He didn't consider

Isaac "holy unto Abraham." When giving God his all, Abraham did not keep Isaac in reserve. He did not *withhold* Isaac.

Paul is repeating those very words from *Torah*, words revered by his Jewish audience, and saying, "He did not even hold His own Son in reserve, but gave Him up as an offering for you. Is that not proof *that all He has* is available to you? God has given you His all. Everything." Do you see? If He loves you so completely that He did not even spare His own Son, could He possibly be reluctant to give you any other thing?

He has given you faith—the ability to access everything He has. All His power. All His provision. Later in the book, you will learn how to put faith to work so that it brings into your circumstances, into your experience, all that God has available.

His gift tells you this about its Giver: He loves you beyond all reason. He loves you beyond all imagination. "He who did not spare his own Son, but gave him up for us all—how will he not also, along with him, *graciously* (freely, joyfully, generously) give us *all* things?" (Romans 8:32, parentheses mine).

Generous

Second, the gift of faith tells you that its Giver is generous, not stingy. He pours out blessing. He doesn't sprinkle it or dribble it. He pours it. He has given us Himself through the Holy Spirit, "whom he poured out on us *generously* through Jesus Christ our Savior" (Titus 3:6). He offers us "the riches of God's grace that he *lavished* on us with all wisdom and understanding" (Ephesians 1:7–8). "How great is the love the Father has *lavished* on us, that we should be called children of God!" (1 John 3:1).

For the Jewish nation, one of the prominent proofs of God's personal provision for their needs was the provision of manna during their desert years. It was the miracle authenticating that God was working through Moses, commonly referred to as "the former redeemer." When "the latter redeemer," the expected Messiah, appeared, the rabbis had taught that a similar authenticating work would be manifested. The Messiah would perform a "work" like that of Moses. Remember the challenge Jesus' audience gave Him? "So they asked him, 'What miraculous sign then will you give that we may see it and believe you? What will you do? Our forefathers ate the manna in the desert; as it is written: "He gave them bread from heaven to eat"'" (John 6:30).

Manna was defined in Jewish thought as "the bread that came down out of heaven." So, in their history, the manna experience was when the provision of heaven entered the environment of earth and gave life, when the substance available in heaven came into the circumstances of earth, when their earthly needs were met with the riches that came out of heaven. When God provided manna, how much did He provide? He promised the people, "in the morning you will be *filled* with bread" (Exodus 16:12). True to His word, the Lord provided. "Each morning everyone gathered as much as he needed" (Exodus 16:21). Every morning, every single person had as much as he needed. Every single day, every single person was filled with bread.

Consider manna. The people had left behind everything they knew and now had become nomads wandering through the barren desert. They needed nutrition to keep them alive. They couldn't plant any crops. They couldn't go to the market. Where would they find the nutrition that would stave off death and give them life? The answer was simple. Every morning, as the Lord instructed, they walked out of their homes and took hold of all that the Lord had provided. Provision was waiting for them every morning. All they had to do was pick it up and use it.

The gift tells you this about its Giver: He is generous—willing and eager to give you everything He has. He makes everything you need available to you. He is a lavish Giver. All the provision of heaven has been made accessible for the circumstances of earth.

Trustworthy

Third, the gift of faith tells you that its Giver is trustworthy and dependable. You can depend on Him. When He invites you to put your trust in Him, there are no caveats. He will always, always—under every circumstance, in every situation, at every moment—be totally in control. This is what He promised and you can count on Him. "And God is able to make *all* grace abound to you, so that in *all* things at *all* times, having *all* that you need, you will *abound* in *every* good work" (2 Corinthians 9:8). The Greek word translated "abound" is *perisseuo* and it means "to superabound; to have excess; to have more than enough."

My niece Amy, when she was a little girl, was staying with my parents. My mother was pouring syrup on her pancakes one morning. When Mom stopped pouring, Amy said, "Put some more." My mother responded, "Oh, I think that's enough." Amy said, "But I don't like enough. I like too much!" When it comes to the things of the Spirit of God, I'm just like Amy. I want too much. I want to superabound. And I can trust God with that desire because He is able to make me overflow and slosh over with His abundance. My son Kennedy preached a message he called "H2O"; it stood for "Here 2 Overflow." It's my motto now. I'm H2O.

He is able. He has the power. He has the know-how. He has the authority. And He *wants* to! Whatever He promises, He can deliver. Abraham was fully persuaded that "God had power to do what he had promised" (Romans 4:21). Every word He speaks contains in it the power to carry it out. In Luke 1:37, the angel says to Mary, "For nothing is impossible with God." A more literal translation is, "For no word from God shall be void of power" (American Standard Version). The verse uses the word *rhema*, which means the voiced word. No *rhema* that God speaks will be powerless. Does Mary's response make more sense now? "'I am the Lord's servant,' Mary answered. "May it be to me as you have *said* [*rhema*]" (Luke 1:38).

God is absolutely dependable. You can trust Him. The Hebrew word for "trust" is the word *batach* and it means to lean your full weight on something else. It pictures leaning on a staff and trusting the staff to hold you up. My 19-year-old son Stinson just had some minor knee surgery yesterday. I'm watching him hobble around on a set of crutches. He leans all of his considerable muscle-bound weight on the crutches and trusts them to carry him. If he were not willing to trust himself to the crutches, he would be stuck in one place. He can only walk by faith. The first steps he took on the crutches were tentative and unsteady, but now he's moving with confidence. By experience, he has learned that he can trust all his weight to the crutches.

You can trust God. You can lean on Him. He will not let you down.

He has given you faith as a gift and the gift tells you this about its Giver: He is trustworthy. He is absolutely solid, absolutely steady. That's the only way faith could work. It only works because God is able.

Sovereign

Fourth, the gift of faith tells you that its Giver is sovereign. Faith brings all the power and provision of God into your circumstances. God guarantees it. Faith will work because God has designed it perfectly. Can God make promises to you about the future if He is not in control of the future? Can God promise to act on your behalf every moment if His actions are dependent on anything other than Himself? Can He invite you to fully trust Him if there will be situations in which His power and His plan can be thwarted? Can He ask you to have confidence in His actions in the present if He does not fully know the future?

> *The LORD Almighty has sworn, "Surely, as I have planned, so it will be, and as I have purposed, so it will stand."*
> —Isaiah 14:24

O Lord, you are my God; I will exalt you and praise your name, for in perfect faithfulness you have done marvelous things, things planned long ago.

—Isaiah 25:1

Have you not heard? Long ago I ordained it. In days of old I planned it; now I have brought it to pass.

—2 Kings 19:25

Are you seeing a pattern? God, the faith-Giver, is in control. He has always been in control, He is in control right now, and He will always be in control. That's why faith in God makes perfect sense.

The gift of faith tells you this about the Giver: He is sovereign. He can make promises and tell you to trust Him because He calls all the shots.

Questions for Discussion

1. What are some gifts that have been given to you that especially remind you of something about the giver?

2. What does the gift of faith tell you about its Giver that particularly inspires hope and expectation in you?

3. Do you feel that you are operating in faith, your native air? Or are you struggling and fighting an uphill battle?

4. Identify areas where you are breathing alien air and recognize that as God's gentle invitation to you to enter His rest and leave behind your flesh-based labor.

Chapter Three

FOCUSED FAITH

"Have faith in God," Jesus answered.

—Mark 11:22

We began in chapter 1 to differentiate between believing in an outcome and having faith in God. Belief in an outcome will let you down. Faith in God never will. Faith is not believing *something*. Faith is believing *Someone*.

Because I want to know truth, I am always willing to listen to and consider all sides of a question. It makes some people anxious to open-mindedly give a hearing to ideas they have been taught are not acceptable, but I am too inquisitive to be satisfied that the truth I accept is truth if I have not poked it and prodded it and shaken it and turned it inside-out. So I'm kind of an adventurous thinker. I just needed to explain that to you as we continue in this journey of discovery. I am in *no way* suggesting that there is any truth outside the Bible, the inspired Word of God without any error. I am in *no way* suggesting that there is any alternative truth worth considering other than Jesus Christ, God in the flesh, crucified, resurrected, and seated at the Father's right hand, the only bridge between God and mankind. But within those parameters, there are many areas to explore.

When a person, including myself, says, "I believe the Bible," what they are really saying is, "I believe the way I interpret the Bible." Can we be honest about that? Two truly born-again Christians, who both love Jesus with equal passion and believe the Bible with equal fervor, can disagree on a variety of points. Each will make her case from the Bible. Each will believe as she does because she is convinced that the Bible says so. Am I right?

You already know that there are many such variants within the Christian community regarding faith—what it is and how it operates. Let me explain to you how my explorations of truth reach a conclusion. As I examine with open mind various thoughts, I eliminate the ones that, on close inspection, won't hold up to all my questioning and testing and pushing and pulling.

Testing Truth

Do you know what a "null hypothesis" is? A hypothesis is a prediction or an assumption about an outcome not yet tested. When you test a hypothesis, you are really testing two hypotheses. One is the outcome you predict, and the second is the other possible outcome. The outcome you hypothesize as true is called the "alternative hypothesis" and the other possibility is called the "null hypothesis." You test the null hypothesis in order to disprove it, therefore leaving the alternative hypothesis as the only option. You don't really know which hypothesis is the truth until you have tested them. You may start out with a strong assumption, but you can't know. By disproving the null hypothesis, you have proven the alternative hypothesis. That's what I do. By disproving some "hypothesis" about faith, I have proven the alternative hypothesis true.

How do I examine a hypothesis? Not by subjective experience alone. I hold it up to the Word of God and let the light shine on it from every angle. I debate myself. I do as the Jewish rabbis encourage and "wrestle with Torah." Most of all, I ask the Spirit of Truth to lead me into all truth, and I have confidence that He will. Then, I put it to the test in my life. I give the living Word free rein and hang on for the ride. And I am in no hurry. I think things through for years, even decades, before I am convinced enough to lay it out as truth. I'm learning every day.

Why did I tell you all that? Because as I share with you what I am convinced beyond all doubt to be true, I want you to know how I reached the conclusions I have reached. I want you to know that there are some null hypotheses along the way—thinking that I have discarded because it did not stand the test. And I will tell you exactly where each null hypothesis fell short.

God-Focused

Again, faith has its full focus on God. That's why you have to know Him. God the Father, God the Son, God the Spirit—the Three who are the One God. You have to trust Him fully. One of the null hypotheses about faith that I have examined and discarded over time is that faith always knows how God will act and latches onto an expected outcome, not making room it its thinking for any other possibility. So, for example, you are diagnosed with an illness. The null hypothesis says, "God never, ever uses physical illness to work out His eternal plans. God fully intends for every believer to have perfect physical health. I have been diagnosed with an illness. I will believe God for complete healing and I won't allow for any other possibility, because that would be doubt or unbelief. If I have doubt or unbelief, then God will not heal me."

Here is how I have discovered that true faith works: I can allow for even the worst-case scenario in any given situation and know that I will be victorious. Do you recall the faith of Shadrach, Meshach, and Abednego recorded in Daniel 3:17–18?

> If we are thrown into the blazing furnace, the God we serve is able to save us from it, and he will rescue us from your hand, O king. But even if he does not, we want you to know, O king, that we will not serve your gods or worship the image of gold you have set up.

They knew that even if the worst possible scenario occurred, God was being faithful. They did not know whether or not they would be thrown into the fire. They did not say, "I'm believing in God to keep me from the fiery furnace." They said, "We trust God, no matter the outcome."

King Nebuchadnezzar, the king of Babylon, where the three young men were captives, had declared himself to be God and had made a law that anyone who did not bow down to his image would be thrown into a fiery furnace. Shadrach, Meshach, and Abednego knew that they would never obey the king's edict. They would never worship Nebuchadnezzar. They also knew that meant that they would face a situation intended to bring a sure and horrific death. They had their confidence so focused on God that they knew that He could keep them from facing the fiery furnace, but that if He did not, it would still have a good outcome. Not only did they not escape the king's punishment, but the fire was heated up seven times hotter than usual. They got the worst of the worst.

Faith is the highest form of reasoning. I know you have heard that faith and reason are polar opposites. Not so. Faith is logic in its purest form. We'll pursue that thought further later. But I am going to challenge you right now to reason and conclude what is true. Let me repeat the point I am making. Faith can allow for the worst-case scenario and still be fearless. Why? Because God is in charge.

Let's pursue the argument, because remember, I've asked all the questions and given this hypothesis about faith a full and fair hearing in my life and I have rejected it as the null hypothesis. Part of this whole logic-package is that if it is good, then God did it, and if it is bad, then God had nothing to do with it. "Don't go blaming God," someone will say. "After all, we live in a fallen world and evil happens." I have a couple of problems with the logic of that position. First, you can't believe half a thought. Do you believe that God sometimes stops evil or bad things from happening? Or do you believe that evil always has its way and operates without interference from God? I think you will say that God sometimes stops evil and overrules disaster. That's the first half of the thought, and I believe it is true. God sometimes intervenes to stop difficulties and disasters. The rest of the thought is this: if He sometimes intervenes to stop bad things from happening, then when He does not stop them, He does not stop them on purpose. Otherwise, when He does not stop bad things from happening, is He then careless? Distracted? Helpless? Can He tell you to trust Him and rest in Him because He is in charge...unless, of course, someone wants to use his or her free will or unless your enemy devises an evil plan against you? Under those circumstances, He is out of the picture.

Do you believe that God sometimes stops evil or bad things from happening? Or do you believe that evil always has its way and operates without interference from God?

Take the next logical step in reasoning out this truth. God is only good. No evil or negative purpose dwells in His heart. He can divert any difficulty or disaster, big or little, and He most often does so. When He does not—when He purposefully allows a difficulty, a challenge, a heartache, a disaster—His purposes are good and loving.

I have had many a person say to me when I discuss this thought, "Well, I can't see any good that could come out of..." and then they go on to describe a terrible and tragic situation. I need to challenge you, then, if this is what you are thinking. Is that the measure? Is that the deciding factor? Whether or not *you* can see? Whether *you* can perceive? My friend, it is not. Faith is knowing that God sees what you cannot. If you could know as God knows—fully, end from beginning, every detail into eternity—you would make the same decisions He has made. Know that for sure.

When you think that faith means deciding on an outcome and blocking all other possibilities out of your mind, you will often be disappointed. You will have to come up with an explanation, and it will most likely be, "I didn't have enough faith."

Some of you are upset with me right now. You are thinking of closing this book and throwing it in the trash, or selling it on eBay. Wait! Don't go yet. Just hear me out, even if only to prove me wrong so you can file this book under "null hypothesis." We are going to get to how faith really does work and how faith brings into our lives the incredible, mind-boggling, beyond-all-comprehension power and provision of God. But it has to be truth, not myth. You will love the truth. The truth will make you free.

Still with me? Okay, then let's continue to examine the Word of God in this matter. The eleventh chapter of Hebrews is a detailed treatise on faith and how it operates. It defines faith, then it puts out for display occurrences of faith in the lives of the ancients. As it comes to its conclusion, the writer of Hebrews says, in Hebrews 11:32–39:

> *And what more shall I say? I do not have time to tell about Gideon, Barak, Samson, Jephthah, David, Samuel and the prophets, who through faith conquered kingdoms, administered justice, and gained what was promised; who shut the mouths of lions, quenched the fury of the flames, and escaped the edge of the sword; whose weakness was turned to strength; and who became powerful in battle and routed foreign armies. Women received back their dead, raised to life again.* [Sounding pretty good? By faith they saw the power and provision of God operate in the circumstances of earth. Keep reading.] *Others were tortured and refused to be released, so that they might gain a better resurrection. Some faced jeers and flogging, while still others were chained and put in prison. They were stoned; they were sawed in two; they were put to death by the sword. They went about in sheepskins and goatskins, destitute, persecuted and mistreated—the world was not worthy of them. They wandered in deserts and mountains, and in caves and holes in the ground.* [Well, maybe they didn't have enough faith. Keep reading.] *These were **all***

*commended for their **faith**, yet none of them received what had been promised.*

The ones whose faith caused them to endure difficulties, heartbreaks, and disasters victoriously were "commended for their faith" right along with those whose faith caused them to escape difficulty, heartbreak, and disaster. The word "commended" means to be put out on display. God put them center-stage as a display of faith. "Look!" He has said to all inhabitants of heaven and earth. "This is what faith looks like."

Let's listen to the apostle Paul: "I have learned to be content whatever the circumstances. I know what it is to be in need, and I know what it is to have plenty. I have learned the secret of being content in any and every situation, whether well fed or hungry, whether living in plenty or in want. I can do everything through him who gives me strength" (Philippians 4:11–13).

Paul learned a secret. This secret caused him to live every moment of every day in a state of contentment. He learned it by experience, not in theory. He learned that the unchanging presence of God satisfied him. It was the same when God allowed adversity in his life as when God supernaturally intervened to circumvent difficulties. All the same.

Let me explain what I think Paul discovered. It starts with realizing how our human nature works. We are all busy trying to arrange outward events in such a way that they will produce inner contentment— a sense of safety, of being loved, of satisfaction. If this would happen, or if that would go away, or if this would change, or if that would stay the same…then we would have the inner contentment. So we think.

Paul learned that it's not what God *does*, but who God *is* that produces contentment. What happened on the outside of him does not add to or subtract from his inner rest. How did he know such a wonderful thing? He *learned* it. How did he learn it? He learned how to be content when he was in need by being in need. How did he learn how to be content while being hungry? He learned by being hungry.

Paul's faith was focused on God, not on an outcome in any given circumstance. Faith knows that God is working toward an outcome that is beyond anything that we could ask or imagine. Faith is "future-focused." *Future-focused* describes a person who is so fully focused on the goal that he is blind to the discouragements along the way, oblivious to the bumps in the road. Faith keeps its eyes on God, who is definitely moving all circumstances in a forward direction, bringing to completion a good and loving work. When He allows difficulties to come into your experience, you can be sure that He is doing something beneficial by means of them and He is doing something He could not accomplish without that very challenge. His plans are always for your benefit. His plans are always well thought out long, long in advance. Let me remind you of something about God: He is very smart.

You will find that once you move to the kind of faith that knows beyond a doubt that no circumstance can defeat you and that every circumstance will work out to your benefit, you will also find that more times than you ever realized, God is diverting difficulties, smoothing the path you are walking, and bringing supernatural supply into your life. You will realize that you can live continually in the assurance that God is working productively in every detail of your life.

Doubt or Unbelief?

Some of you are thinking, "But the Scriptures say that I must not doubt, because if I doubt I will receive nothing from the Lord. So if I don't latch onto a belief in an outcome and discipline my mind to believe it, then I am doubting. What about that, Jennifer Kennedy Dean?" I'm glad you asked.

"But when he asks, he must believe and not doubt, because he who doubts is like a wave of the sea, blown and tossed by the wind. That man should not think he will receive anything from the Lord; he is a double-minded man, unstable in all he does" (James 1:6–8). These statements from the Book of James have discouraged and intimidated many a believer. Don't take these words out of their context. Under the inspiration of the Holy Spirit, James wrote a letter, not a series of isolated, unrelated statements. You can only understand these sentences in their context. Read the whole thought.

> *Consider it pure joy, my brothers, whenever you face trials of many kinds, because you know that the testing of your faith develops perseverance. Perseverance must finish its work so that you may be mature and complete, not lacking anything. If any of you lacks wisdom, he should ask God, who gives generously to all without finding fault, and it will be given to him. But when he asks, he must believe and not doubt, because he who doubts is like a wave of the sea, blown and tossed by the wind. That man should not think he will receive anything from the Lord; he is a double-minded man, unstable in all he does.*
>
> —James 1:2–8

What is James addressing? He is talking about when you face a difficulty of any kind. What are you to do first in any difficulty? You are to consider it "pure joy." The Greek words suggest cheerfulness, unmixed with any anxiety. *All* joy. Why? Because you are future-focused. You know that any difficulty is in place to move you to the next level of blessing and maturity. You keep your eyes on the prize. He goes on to tell you what the process is producing. Perseverance—steadiness, sure-footedness, staying power. Then he says, in essence, "While you are going through this trial, you need wisdom. You need to know how to live according to the truth you know. So ask for the wisdom that comes from God." Here's what I see from this: wisdom is something that comes to me from God—something He gives me. I don't have wisdom unless God gives it to me. If I try to figure out my situation and analyze it and scope it, I will fall short. The Greek term here for "fall short" is a banking term that means to run short of funds. Wisdom is that which God alone possesses and God alone can give. When I ask Him for it, He gives it to me—freely, generously, willingly, *immediately*. A direct transfer from His mind to mine. The "getting" is simultaneous with the asking. He is rich in wisdom. His wisdom is mine for the asking.

Then James says, "But when he asks, he must believe and not doubt." Let me restate it: "When he asks for wisdom in the midst of difficulties, he must believe that God will make a direct transfer into his mind and he must not keep second-guessing. He must act according to what God has deposited in him and not waver back and forth between his fear-based thinking and the wisdom that God—who is true to His word—has faithfully supplied." (We'll deal later with the ways that God speaks and reveals Himself to you.)

Then James says that the person who asks for wisdom *para Theos*—from God—must act on that wisdom. Otherwise he will not receive anything *para Kurios*—from the Lord. Same wording, obviously tying the two thoughts together. The word translated "receive" is *lambano*. It means "to take hold of, to catch." It is an action taken. So the Lord will give wisdom, but if the person does not take hold of the wisdom, then he will be vacillating and unstable. The person must receive what the Lord gives. That is exactly what faith does. It receives what the Lord gives.

So, James is not saying that you must settle on an expected outcome and force all doubt about that outcome from your mind. James is saying that you must have faith in God.

Unbelief is something different from doubt. Unbelief will keep you from going to God with your needs in the first place. Unbelief will cause you to intentionally dismiss God in favor of your own abilities. Read in Hebrews 3:19 the effect of unbelief: "So we see that they were not able to enter, because of their unbelief." Review the incident to which this verse refers. You will find it in Numbers 13:17–14:4.

As the Israelites arrived at the border of the land that God had promised them, Moses sent twelve men in to get a feel for the situation. When they came back, ten of the twelve reported that there were giants in the land and that the Israelites would be like grasshoppers to them. The people decided to let their fear direct their decisions. I want you to be clear about this situation. The Israelites did not wonder whether or not God had led them to the land or whether or not God was telling them to go into the land. That was a given. But they did not have faith *in God*. They refused to trust God. Listen to them whine: "That night all the people of the community raised their voices and wept aloud. All the Israelites grumbled against Moses and Aaron, and the whole assembly said to them, 'If only we had died in Egypt! Or in this desert! *Why is the LORD bringing us to this land* only to let us fall by the sword? Our wives and children will be taken as plunder. Wouldn't it be better for us to go back to Egypt?' And they said to each other, 'We should choose a leader and go back to Egypt'" (Numbers 14:1–4). Here is unbelief— choosing to believe their own perceptions and intentionally not trusting God. Refusing, intentionally and rebelliously, not to obey God because they did not have faith in Him. They lined themselves up with the enemy's lies and agreed with fear. They had faith—but not in God. They put their faith in fear and trusted that failure would be the result of obeying God.

You might experience feelings of uncertainty. You might wonder if things are going to work out. You might have an emotion of fear or anxiety. But it is not unbelief unless you deliberately decide against what you know God wants.

The first step toward using the faith that God has given you is to receive from God that which He has given you. You have to open your life to allow His gift to have room to move around and work its way into your spirit-cells and let it soak into your life. He has given faith to you. It's in you. But you have to accept it and use it. Remember the manna? God made it available. God put it into their lives. But they had to walk out every morning and collect it and use it.

I have a wonderful way to grocery shop. I was designed for the age of the Internet. I even use it to shop for groceries. I get online and go to my grocery store's Web site. Once there, I type in my secret code. Then I shop! I tell them everything I want and I pay with my bankcard. At the grocery store, they gather up my order and have it all ready for me. It's mine. It's paid for. It's set aside and waiting for me. But until I go to the store and turn in my receipt, it is not in my possession, ready for my use.

Faith is yours. It's paid for. It's set aside and waiting for you. But you have to take hold of it and put it to work. Remember, it is a gift from God and He doesn't skimp. You have *huge* faith available to you. More than enough.

The more we understand about the nature of faith, the more we will understand about how to put it to work. When you get to the third section of this book, "Faith: The Function," you will consider in detail how faith operates. I know that's what you want to know, and don't worry, that's where we are headed. I keep alluding to it as we put the pieces together, so I want you to be assured that everything is aimed at that goal.

Right now, stop and let this truth make a little nest for itself in your heart. Let it settle in. Embrace it. Say this. Write it down in your prayer journal and sign your name to it: "I believe that God has freely given me tremendous, earth-changing, mountain-moving faith and that He will teach me how to use it to access all of His power and all of His provision."

Questions for Discussion

1. Why can faith allow for the worst-case scenario?

2. What is the difference between doubt and unbelief?

3. If your faith is focused on God, is there anything in His character that would cause you to feel unsettled or unsafe?

FAITH:
THE FOUNDATION

Chapter Four

HOW FIRM A FOUNDATION

*Being fully persuaded that God had power to do **what he had promised**.*
—Romans 4:21

Faith has a foundation, a resting place. The word of God is faith's birthplace. God Himself is the focus of faith, and His word is the way that He reveals Himself to us. His word is the method by which He discloses His innermost thoughts; by His word, His mind—His reasoning, His purposes, His desires—becomes accessible to us.

The wonderful old hymn says:

> How firm a foundation, ye saints of the Lord,
> Is laid for your faith in His excellent Word!
> What more can He say than to you He hath said,
> To you who for refuge to Jesus have fled?
> —"How Firm a Foundation," words from John Rippon's *Selection of Hymns*, 1787

God's word lays an excellent foundation for your faith. In His word, He proclaims what He intends to do and describes what He has available to give. Unless we interact with His living word continually, our faith will have nowhere to put down roots.

His word found in the Bible is living, active, powerful, creative. It is not stagnant and static. God is a speaking God, who is always speaking in the present tense. The Scripture opens and the One True God is introduced to mankind as a speaking God, speaking words that create life and order. "In the beginning God created the heavens and the earth. Now the earth was formless and empty, darkness was over the surface of the deep, and the Spirit of God was hovering over the waters. And God said, 'Let there be light,' and there was light" (Genesis 1:1–3). Hebrew Torah scholars teach that what God reveals first is what is primary and foundational. What is revealed subsequently must be understood as building upon the first mention. The very first mention of God tells us that He is a creating God who does His work by His now-speaking word. Light came into being at His word—at the moment of His speaking, as immediate response to His voice. Every living thing exists because of the word that proceeded from the mouth of God.

God Himself is the focus of faith, and His word is the way that He reveals Himself to us.

As Jesus faced down His enemy in the desert, remember that Jesus referred to "every word that proceeds out of the mouth of God" (Matthew 4:4 NASB). Jesus is quoting the Scripture and He no doubt said it either in the Hebrew in which it was written, or in the Aramaic language (closely akin to Hebrew) that Jesus and His contemporaries spoke. The Greek wording in the oldest Greek renderings available to us says something like, "Every single *rhema* (present, voiced word) that flows like a river through the mouth of God." The Greek word *ekporeuomai*—"flows out of or comes forth from"—is in the present tense and active voice. It is happening in real time. Right now. At this moment. Man lives by the words that God is speaking right now.

Let's look at the Scripture Jesus was quoting: "man does not live on bread alone but on every word that comes from the mouth of the LORD" (Deuteronomy 8:3). In Hebrew culture, most Jewish people knew much of the Scripture by heart. It was a common way of

communicating when a person would quote a portion of a Scripture, or the opening words and the closing words of a passage, implying the whole passage. It would be like when one person steeped in American culture and language says to another, "If the shoe fits," or, "When in Rome." Confident of his hearer's familiarity with the phrase, the speaker would be communicating the entire phrase by stating a portion of it. When Jesus spoke those words to His enemy, He was implying the whole thought. Let's look at it.

"He humbled you, causing you to hunger and then feeding you with manna, which neither you nor your fathers had known, to teach you that man does not live on bread alone but on every word that comes from the mouth of the LORD" (Deuteronomy 8:3). God put the Israelites in a position where they would experience hunger *so that* He could feed them with manna *for the purpose of* teaching them that they could live on what flows from the mouth of God. What was manna? It was the bread that came out of heaven and caused them to live. In the Hebrew, "word" is not in the text Deuteronomy 8:3; it has been inserted by translators. The Hebrew says, "...by every single thing, every sort of thing, that flows like a river through the mouth of God." What proceeded from the mouth of God? Manna! That's right, manna came from the mouth of God. Somewhere in the heavens, God said, "Let there be manna," and there was manna. Manna was the spoken word of God in an earth form. Manna existed because God spoke it. The Israelites lived by the manna that God spoke into being—the word that proceeded out of His mouth.

Jesus had just spent forty days and forty nights fasting in the desert. He was saying to His enemy, "God has allowed Me to experience the reality that My spirit and My innermost being is nourished and given life by what God is feeding Me—His living word voiced to Me in the present tense. Everything that My body needs, God will speak into My life."

Your faith is resting on the foundation of the word of God. But don't make the mistake of confining your idea of the word of God to some-

thing He said in the past and that continues to have relevance today. The word of God is something He is always speaking in the present tense. His word is living and active and now.

The Scripture is the living Word of God, so even those passages addressed to a particular audience in a specific time regarding a unique event have layers of meaning. Even those passages that are spoken within the context of time echo into eternity, speaking fresh truth to God's people in any given moment.

The word that God is speaking comes to us, according to Scripture, by three means. We will examine each carefully. The three conduits by which God communicates are (1) the living, indwelling Jesus, communicated by the Holy Spirit, (2) the written Word we call the Scripture, and (3) His creation.

The Nature of God's Word

As we start to look closely at God's word, keep in mind the nature of His word. First, remember that it is flowing right out of the depths of God. Second, remember that anything that God speaks is brought into being by the very act of His speaking. If God says, "Let there be light," there is light. If He says, "Let there be manna," there is manna. And third, remember that His word is eternal and it is "the last word." Nothing can override it or undermine it. His word is the "amen" to all His promises—the "it is so; so let it be."

Through His word, God intends to reveal His will to us. He means for us to know what is available and what He desires to put into our lives. It is not His plan to keep us in the dark, but instead He wants to bring us into His inner circle, where He can tell us His secrets. Listen to Jesus say this to you right now: "I no longer call you servants, because a servant does not know his master's business. Instead, I have called you friends, for *everything* that I learned from my Father I have made known to you" (John 15:15–16).

Let's look at the eternal record and see what is proceeding from the mouth of God about knowing His desires.

First, read 1 John 5:14–15 and look for the key to experiencing consistently the power and provision of God in response to your prayers. "This is the confidence we have in approaching God: that if we ask anything according to his will, he hears us. And if we know that he hears us—whatever we ask—we know that we have what we asked of him." Do you see? We can have absolute and unwavering confidence that we have what we asked for *when we know we are asking according to His will.*

Is there a catch? Is this just a bait and switch? If God says that the key to answered prayer is to ask according to His will, then He must have made it possible to know His will.

For a moment, ignore that thought screaming at you, "How can a human being ever presume to know God's will? How presumptuous! Where is the humility?" If I recognize in myself a belief that is embedded in my doctrine, but which is contradicted by the whole Scripture, it is uncomfortable for me at first. And I don't let it go lightly. So I don't want you to let anything go lightly. Think it through, asking the Spirit to lead you into all the truth, and don't be afraid to poke and prod truth. It will hold its own. So if you are uncomfortable right now, that is not a problem. Scripture is the only source to count on, so we are examining the Scripture.

God's will is a mystery, but it is a mystery that He has revealed. In Colossians 1:25–26, Paul says that God had given him a commission "to present to you the word of God in its fullness—the mystery that has been kept hidden for ages and generations, but is now disclosed to the saints." Paul is saying that the abundant riches that God has available had been disguised or hidden or kept secret for ages and generations. He had intentionally not allowed the fullness of His provision to be known. But all that has changed. Now the Word of God (Paul means the Old Testament) can be announced in its fullness—all the layers exposed and all the pictures brought to life. "To them God has chosen to make known among the Gentiles the glorious riches of this mystery, which is Christ in you, the hope of glory" (Colossians 1:27). The mystery and all its fullness and all its abundance is summed up in these three words: Christ in you. You could summarize this passage of Paul's letter like this: God's will that was once hidden is now revealed.

Time and time again, Scripture refers to the mystery of His will, once hidden, but now revealed. In Romans, Paul talks about "the revelation of the mystery hidden for long ages past, but now revealed and made known through the prophetic writings by the command of the eternal God, so that all nations might believe and obey him." (Romans 16:25–26). The prophetic writings were in place, but the deep mystery of God's will contained in them has only been revealed since the Spirit came to indwell believers. The mystery of His will is now revealed.

"But," you say, "those Scriptures are just saying that God wants us to know His plan for our eternal salvation. They are not referring to knowing God's will on a daily basis." Are you sure? Look at Paul's prayer recorded in the book of Colossians: "so that they may have the *full riches of complete understanding,* in order that they may know the mystery of God, namely, Christ, *in whom are hidden all the treasures of wisdom and knowledge*" (Colossians 2:2–3). Once you have Christ and have come to understand God's plan—His revealed mystery of Christ in you—then you have access to all the wisdom and knowledge of God, because God's will is embodied in Jesus. You've got Jesus? Then you have the storehouse of all the desires of God. Your salvation includes everything about your new, eternal quality of life. Your salvation is not just what happens to you after your body dies.

Let me relieve your anxiety right now and assure you that I am not saying that you or any human will ever know the detailed way that God will bring His will into being. The path His will takes, the way He brings His will into being, remains a mystery. "Oh, the depth of the riches of the wisdom and knowledge of God! How unsearchable his judgments, and his paths beyond tracing out!" (Romans 11:33). God will never hand over to us His all-knowingness. Sometimes we mistake His "will" for His "ways" and become confused. When I think that I have reached an understanding of God's will and begin to pray according to it, He often begins bringing that *will* about in a *way* that looks to me like a mistake. I have now built up enough history with Him that usually I know to wait and watch—not to confuse His ways with His will. I'm learning not to confuse *what* He's doing with *how* He's doing it.

But back to the question at hand. Can I know God's will? Does God want me to understand what He desires?

God wants you to understand His will. He wants you to have "the full riches of *complete understanding*" (Colossians 2:2). He has given His Spirit so that "we may *understand* what God has freely given us" (1 Corinthians 2:12). Jesus has come and "has given us *understanding,* so that we may know him who is true"

Sometimes we mistake His "will" for His "ways" and become confused.

(1 John 5:20). He wants to "*fill* you with the knowledge of his will through *all spiritual wisdom and understanding*" (Colossians 1:9). We live in the fullness of God's grace, which He "lavished on us with *all wisdom and understanding*" (Ephesians 1:8). He wants us to have "a *full understanding* of every good thing we have in Christ" (Philemon 6).

Does it sound as if God is keeping His will a secret? On the contrary, He has made every provision for you to know His will. He wants you to know His will. He invites you to know His will. In fact, understanding His will is the cornerstone of faith. You won't be able to exercise faith unless you understand what the word of God has revealed to be available. You cannot walk in the power of prayer if you do not pray according to His will. Since He intends for prayer to be the conduit that brings His power to earth, and since He designs all things perfectly, He plans for you to know His will.

The Deep Things of God

In 1 Corinthians 2:6–16, Paul explains how you and I can know the deep things of God. Before we start digesting these words, let me point you to Paul's Jewish understanding of the deep things of God. "He reveals deep and hidden things; he knows what lies in darkness, and light dwells with him" (Daniel 2:22). God knows truth that is deep (unsearchable) and hidden (kept secret). He alone knows these deep truths. At moments of His own choosing, He reveals those deep and hidden things to individuals.

Paul, writing out of his Jewish mindset, says:

> *We do, however, speak a message of wisdom among the mature, but not the wisdom of this age or of the rulers of this age, who are coming to nothing. No, we speak of God's **secret wisdom**, a wisdom that **has been hidden** and that God destined for our glory before time began. None of the rulers of this age understood it, for if they had, they would not have crucified the Lord of glory. However, as it is written:*
>
> *"No eye has seen,*
> *no ear has heard,*
> *no mind has conceived*
> *what God has prepared for those who love him"—*
> *but God has revealed it to us by his Spirit.*
>
> *The Spirit searches all things, even **the deep things of God**. For who among men knows the thoughts of a man except the man's spirit within him? In the same way no one knows the thoughts of God except the Spirit of God. We have not received the spirit of the world but the Spirit who is from God, **that we may understand what God has freely given us**. This is what we speak, not in words taught us by human wisdom but in words taught by the Spirit, expressing spiritual truths in spiritual words. The man without the Spirit does not accept the things that come*

from the Spirit of God, for they are foolishness to him, and he cannot understand them, because they are spiritually discerned. The spiritual man makes judgments about all things, but he himself is not subject to any man's judgment:

"For who has known the mind of the Lord
*   that he may instruct him?"*
But we have the mind of Christ.

—1 Corinthians 2:6–16

Paul says (my paraphrase), "I am speaking words to you that explain the wisdom that God has imparted to me about the deep and hidden things. This wisdom is completely divorced from what passes as wisdom among the rulers of this age—transient, time-framed thought rather than eternal truth. These God-authored words I'm speaking are bringing to light that which has been obscured since time began. This secret wisdom has always been destined for us, meant to bring us into glory by the indwelling life of Christ." Then he continues, explaining New Covenant reality. "The very things that have been hidden—the very things that no eye has seen, no ear has heard, and no mind has conceived—have now been revealed to us by the Spirit, who knows the depths of God. He instructs us in all the secret wisdom of the heavenly realms for this purpose: so that we will *understand what is available to us*—what God wills us to have."

Are you getting excited about this? I'm about ready to break into a dance of some sort. God wants to reveal to you His deepest thoughts, tell you His best secrets. He wants to instruct you in His will, fill you with the knowledge of His will.

God's word—His eternal, powerful, living word—is His tool for revealing His heart and desires to you. He speaks His word in the present tense to you. It lays a firm foundation for your faith.

In the following chapters, let's look at the three forms His word takes.

1. How does God's Word provide the firm foundation for your faith?

2. Are you convinced that God wants you to know His desires?

3. What is the difference between knowing what He wants to do and knowing how He wants to do it?

4. If you relinquish the need to know *how* He will bring His will into being, and rest in the reality that He *is* bringing His will about, what will change in your daily walk?

Chapter Five

GOD'S LIVING WORD

The Word became flesh and made his dwelling among us.

—John 1:14

John opens his Gospel with the very words that open the Scripture: "at the beginning" (a more accurate translation of the Hebrew than the more commonly seen "in the beginning"). What John says is this: "When the beginning of creating occurred, the Word already was." By opening his message with this most Hebraic phrasing and concept, John, I am convinced, shows that his whole message is to be interpreted in light of Hebrew concepts rather than Greek concepts. When interpreting the Greek word *logos* as "word," rather than understanding it in light of Greek concepts of *logos*, we should instead look at the Hebrew concept that was clearly in John's mind. When the thought is translated from the Hebrew—not just the language, but also the mindset—into the Greek language, *logos* is the Greek word that most closely conveys the Hebrew intent.

John was boldly and clearly tying his introduction directly to the opening scenes of creation and the first words of Torah. This was not subtle. John meant for that connection to be made with no ambiguity. So isn't it only logical that his whole approach is placed into a Hebrew setting, especially considering that he was Jewish and the story he is telling is of the Hebrew God and His Messiah? With that in mind, let me take you into the Hebrew concept of "word."

Realizing that John deliberately directed his readers to the creation account, let's look at the Hebrew used in Torah, the creation narrative in Genesis.

> *In the beginning God created the heavens and the earth. Now the earth was formless and empty, darkness was over the surface of the deep, and the Spirit of God was hovering over the waters.*
>
> *And God **said** ['amar], "Let there be light," and there was light. God saw that the light was good, and he separated the light from the darkness. God called the light "day," and the darkness he called "night." And there was evening, and there was morning— the first day.*
>
> —Genesis 1:1–5

The Hebrew word *'amar* is translated here "said." Its root means "to make visible" or "to be visible." The etymology of the word then develops into "to make plain" and then to "say" (*Theological Wordbook of the Old Testament*, volume 1, page 54). When God says, "Let there be light," light becomes visible.

John ties the incarnation of Jesus the Messiah directly to this Torah passage. That which has always been—the Word—is, at a point in time, made visible. The Word "makes plain"—explains—the invisible One. "No one has ever seen God, but God the One and Only, who is at the Father's side, has *made him known*" (John 1:18).

The Hebrew word most often translated "word" is *dabar*, and it is closely related to *'amar* ("to say"). This is the word that is most often used in the Old Testament text as the basic noun for "word" and its verb form for "speaking" (*Theological Wordbook of the Old Testament*, volume 1, page 179). The Ten Commandments, for example, are the ten *dᵉbarîm*. No doubt, then, it was the Hebrew word in John's mind when he wrote, "In the beginning was the Word, and the Word was with God, and the Word was God.... The Word became flesh and made his dwelling among us" (John 1:1, 14).

The Hebrew word *dabar* and the Greek word *logos* have similar meanings, and the Greek word *logos* was chosen as the best representation of the Hebrew concept being communicated. Both words have a sense of collecting or lining up or cataloging. Both words mean the outward form by which inward thought is expressed. Both have a central concept of logic or reasoning. What is logic? It is the lining up of thoughts in an orderly progression. Logic is stacking truth upon truth until it reaches a conclusion. Both *logos* and *dabar* hint at collecting and lining up words into an explanation, communicating not only the thoughts, but also the reasoning behind them.

Jesus is the *dabar* of God. Not only was He existent at the beginning, but He caused the beginning. "Through him all things were made; without him nothing was made that has been made" (John 1:3).

The person of Jesus the Messiah embodies fully the word of God. He *is* the Word. He is the living Word that the written Word conveys, not the other way around. If there were no living Word, then there would be no written Word to express Him. Without the eternal living Word, there would be no word to be spoken. Because He *is*, therefore everything that exists *is*. "Without him nothing was made that has been made" (John 1:3). The writer of Hebrews refers to the Son, "through whom he made the universe" (Hebrews 1:2). Paul describes Him this way: "by him all things were created: things in heaven and on earth, visible and invisible, whether thrones or powers or rulers or authorities; all things were created by him and for him. He is before all things, and in him all things hold together" (Colossians 1:16–17).

The Word has always been. The Word is. The Word will always be. And the Word lives in you. "The word is near you; it is in your mouth and in your heart" (Romans 10:8).

Everything that comes out of the heart and mind of God is housed in Jesus, and Jesus is housed in you. What is the mystery that was kept hidden in the prophetic writings and revealed only in the New

Covenant? What has God always been saying? What was the content of the Scripture from the beginning? Let me remind you.

> *I have become its servant by the commission God gave me to present to you the word of God in its fullness—the mystery that has been kept hidden for ages and generations, but is now disclosed to the saints. To them God has chosen to make known among the Gentiles the glorious riches of this mystery, which is **Christ in you**, the hope of glory.*
>
> —Colossians 1:25–27

Mystery revealed in you. The Word dwelling in you. The Word speaking in you. The Word by which the universe was created makes His home in you. True to His nature, He is speaking truth and wisdom to you from inside you.

When you read the written Word, the living Word speaks it to you. He speaks to you in present and specific ways, heart to heart. He presents His thoughts to your mind in a fashion that is tailored to your personality and experiences. For example, my friend Libby is an artist. Jesus speaks often to her through colors because she thinks a lot about colors. My friend Mary is a master gardener, and Jesus speaks often to her in gardening metaphors because she knows a lot about gardening. I am a left-brained logical person and Jesus speaks to me in logic and thought sequences. For all of us, He is right there in our present moment speaking life-altering truth in a direct transfer from His mind to ours. Why can He do that? Because "we have the mind of Christ" (1 Corinthians 2:16). Putting the meaning of the Greek words into the sentence, it says something like this: We have as our own possession the thoughts, intellect, judgment, and perceptions of Messiah. We have Messiah's thoughts in a present state—as He thinks them right now—as they are relevant to your moment and to your life.

God's Revelation Through Jesus

God has fully revealed Himself through Jesus. The word *logos* also means a declaration or a message. I've always thought it was interesting that God called Jesus the Message instead of the Messenger. A messenger is separate from the message. Once a messenger has delivered the message, he is no longer relevant. However, Jesus *is* the Message. He always has been the Message and always will be the Message. Apart from the living Jesus, the mind, heart, and thoughts of God have no expression. They are inaccessible.

Suppose that you wanted to know my desires. In order for you to know my will or my desires, I would have to express my thoughts to you. Unless you know what I think, you cannot possibly know what I desire.

What would give you access to my thoughts? How do I put my thoughts into a form that makes them knowable? Words! When I express my thoughts in words, then my thoughts and my words are exactly the same thing. My words are the *exact representation* of my thoughts. If you want to know my thoughts, listen to my words. God speaks to us only one way—by the Son, who is "the *exact representation* of his being" (Hebrews 1:3). The Father and the Son are one, as certainly as my thoughts and my words are one.

God communicates His will through Jesus. Where is Jesus? Jesus is in heaven and on earth. His life links the two ends of the continuum and brings heaven onto earth and earth into heaven.

Jesus: Where Heaven and Earth Meet

Jesus is in heaven. He is seated at the right hand of the Father in the heavenly realms as Paul states in Ephesians 1:20. Because I am in Him, I am seated at the right hand of God and am the recipient of every spiritual blessing heaven holds. "Praise be to the God and Father of our Lord Jesus Christ, who has blessed us in the heavenly realms with every spiritual blessing in Christ" (Ephesians 1:3).

Paul writes in Ephesians 1:13 that when you trusted in Christ, at that moment you were "included in Him" or "placed in Him" and then "sealed into Him" by the Holy Spirit. The expression Paul uses, "sealed in him" (NASB), pictures a king or ruler who places his seal on a letter, marking it with his signet ring. This seal insured that the letter could not be opened except by the appropriate person. The seal effectively secured the letter in its container. You have been sealed into Christ.

My life is hidden in His, Paul tells us in Colossians 3:3: "Your life is now hidden with Christ in God." Wherever Jesus is, I am. I am *in Him*. I am clothed with Him. His precious, perfect life has become my covering because I have taken up residence in Him.

I believe that the following description would accurately depict the scene in heaven's throne room: Jesus, continual and perfect intercessor who intercedes only according to God's will, is before the Father. He is interceding. Where am I, the intercessor on earth, in this scene? I am inside Jesus. Picture this. In the spiritual realm, I am presenting my petitions through His mouth. When I pray, my words reach the Father's ears through the Son.

But in the material realm, on earth, He is living *in me*. "I in them and you in me" (John 17:23). In John 15, Jesus tells me that His life will flow through me like the vine's life flows through the branch. This is a fact woven through the entire New Covenant: Christ is in me. I no longer live, but Christ lives in me. "I have been crucified with Christ and I no longer live, but *Christ lives in me*" (Galatians 2:20).

For the transactions of faith that occur in the earth end of the continuum, He has clothed Himself in me. He expresses His power through me. He expresses His life through my earth-body. My body becomes the vehicle through which He does His work. Prayer from the earth-view looks like this: I am praying. Where is Jesus in this scene? He is *in me*. He is speaking through my mouth. His thoughts are in my mind; His words are in my mouth; His desires are in my heart.

In both ends of the continuum, Jesus is the power. I am always expressing Him. In both realities, I in Him and He in me, He is the life. His life is the animating force in both settings. When we pray, both scenes are occurring simultaneously. Jesus brings the spirit realm into the earth realm and the earth realm into the spirit realm.

The Word of God, the expression of His heart and will, is a living person whose life is my life. God continues to speak His Word through Jesus. In order to understand the Father's revelation of His will, I have to trust the present-tense life of the living Jesus in me, and my present-tense life in the living Jesus.

The living, indwelling Jesus is being communicated to me by the Spirit. Look at what Jesus said in John 16:12–15, describing the Holy Spirit's role once He came to live on the inside of believers.

> *I have much more to say to you, more than you can now bear. But when he, the Spirit of truth, comes, he will guide you into all truth. He will not speak on his own; he will speak only what he hears, and he will tell you what is yet to come. He will bring glory to me by taking from what is mine and making it known to you. All that belongs to the Father is mine. That is why I said the Spirit will take from what is mine and make it known to you.*

What did Jesus mean when He said to His disciples, "I have much more to say to you, more than you can now bear"? He is saying that He had much more that He Himself wanted to say to them. He had more to say, but He couldn't say it at that moment. Why not? Because it was too deep for them. They, on their own, did not have the power to bear it. The Greek says, "You are without the power or ability (*dunamis*) to pick it up and carry it." The Greek word *dunamis* means supernatural power. It will take the very power of God indwelling the in the person of the Holy Spirit for them to be able to take hold of His words.

Jesus continues, "But..." He is contrasting two ideas. He can't tell them more right now, *but* when the Holy Spirit comes, then Jesus can tell them. The Holy Spirit will "guide you into all truth." The word "guide" means to teach or instruct or direct. Its root means a path or a way. The Hebrew thought that the Greek is expressing is probably akin to the word *torah*, which means instruction, guidance, a hand pointing the way.

Jesus says (my paraphrase), "I can't teach you right now, but I can teach you later—when you have My mind in you, when My Spirit can deliver My thoughts to you. My Spirit will speak My thoughts in you. My Spirit will speak to You everything He hears Me say."

This reminds me of the way that God spoke to the Hebrew people and to the Egyptian Pharaoh through Moses and Aaron. Remember that Moses was unable to speak fluently, so God instructed Moses to speak through Aaron. "You [Moses] shall speak to him [Aaron] and put words in his mouth; I will help both of you speak and will teach you what to do. He [Aaron] will speak to the people for you [Moses], and it will be as if he were your mouth and as if you were God to him" (Exodus 4:15–17). Isn't that interesting? God will speak to Moses. Moses will put those words into Aaron's mouth, and Aaron "will not speak on his own; he will speak only what he hears" (John 16:13). "You will be as God to him," God told Moses. In other words, Moses will speak through Aaron in the same way that God speaks through Moses. God spoke through Moses and Moses spoke through Aaron. Throughout the account of their confrontations with the Pharaoh, it is "Moses and Aaron" said, or "Moses and Aaron" did. It was Moses' words being spoken through Aaron's mouth, but it was considered as Moses speaking.

Return your attention to the passage at hand, John 16:12–15. Jesus goes on to say that everything the Father knows, Jesus knows. And the Spirit will take what Jesus knows and declare it to you. Go back now and read the passage again, considering each phrase and how one thought flows into the next. Do you see the whole thing?

Jesus is the Word of God. He is always speaking to you from within. He speaks the Scripture into a present reality. He speaks personal and specific words of promise to you. He creates in you the desires of God for you. "For it is God who works *in you* to will and to act according to his good purpose" (Philippians 2:13).

Jesus, alive in you, provides the firm foundation for your faith.

Questions for Discussion

1. What do you think about this statement: "The written Word is the revelation of the living Word"? What do you take that to mean?

2. What does it mean to you right now, in terms of your current circumstances, to have Jesus living in you?

3. How does the living, indwelling, present Jesus provide a firm foundation for your faith?

Chapter Six

THE WRITTEN WORD

All Scripture is God-breathed and is useful for teaching, rebuking, correcting and training in righteousness, so that the man of God may be thoroughly equipped for every good work.

—2 Timothy 3:16–17

The Scripture is the written form of the living Word. All Scripture is God-breathed, which is the literal meaning of the word "inspired." As always, let's observe the Hebrew concept that the Greek word is representing. We find it first in Torah in the Book of Genesis.

> *In the beginning God created the heavens and the earth. Now the earth was formless and empty, darkness was over the surface of the deep, and the Spirit [ruwach] of God was hovering over the waters.*
>
> —Genesis 1:1–2

The Hebrew word *ruwach* means either "breath" or "wind." It is used regularly to denote the life force of a person. It is the word used for spirit, and "Holy Spirit" or "Spirit of God" in Hebrew is *ruah qodesh* or *ruah YHWH*. The Holy Spirit is God's breath. When a person speaks, he forces breath over his vocal chords to create voice, so that his words will be heard. A person's breath carries his words and delivers them.

If I were to blow, or to breathe out, and if you were to capture my breath in a test tube, you would find my DNA in it. I would have exhaled "me." The Hebrew concept of breath is very strongly rooted in this perception. God was breathing or blowing breath over the earth, which was "wild and waste" (Everett Fox, *The Five Books of Moses*, New York: Schocken, 1997) or "formless and empty." His Spirit was hovering over the waters. What was the result? Life and order. His breath carried His Word into being. He said (projected a word by means of breath) "Let there be light," and light became. So one aspect of the Hebrew concept of "God-breathed" is that Scripture has the very essence of God in it, the power to bring into being that which is not.

The second place in Torah that we see the power of God breathing is in Genesis 2:7: "The LORD God formed the man from the dust of the ground and breathed into his nostrils the breath of life, and the man became a living being." Here the Hebrew word is a different but closely related word, *napah*. You see the same concept: God breathes out of Himself and into the human, and life results.

The Scripture is God-breathed. It came directly out of God and has the power and life of God in it.

The Scripture does not have the power and life of God in it as it sits in printed form on pages bound in books, but only as it comes into contact with the human heart. As we take in the words of Scripture, at that moment the *Ruah* of God is breathing life into it and speaking its life-filled words into our lives, transforming our formless emptiness into life and order.

As you take in Scripture consistently, there will be times when you will feel and sense and experience the life flowing into your mind as new thoughts are awakened, or stale doctrine comes to life, or insight or wisdom seem to flow from its pages into your understanding. Other times, you will not feel the life. There will be times when the contact with God's breathed-out Word is just steady and solid. Either way, God's Word is doing what He said it would do.

God does His work by His Word. When God speaks, His Word is the instrument of His work.

As the rain and snow come down from heaven, and do not return to it without watering the earth and making it bud and flourish, so that it yields seed for the sower and bread for the eater, so is my word that goes out from my mouth: It will not return to me empty, but will accomplish what I desire and achieve the purpose for which I sent it.

—Isaiah 55:10–11

Do you see how God talks about His Word? He says that He sends His Word out with an assignment and that His Word always accomplishes His desires and achieves His purposes. His Word accomplishes His work. His Word waters and nourishes the lives into which He sends it and makes them bud and flourish. He always does His work by His Word. When you are taking in God's Word, it is doing God's work.

Jesus, while in His physical body on earth, once said, "These words you hear are not my own; they belong to the Father who sent me" (John 14:24*b*). Jesus was speaking words that God spoke through Him. He was saying God's words. He described the words He spoke this way: "The words I have spoken to you are spirit and they are life" (John 6:63*b*). The very same kind of breathed-out words that God spoke in the beginning, through which He created all matter and mass and every cell and molecule that exists, is the same kind of words He is speaking to you right now—Spirit and life.

Are you seeing that you can't separate the living Word from the written Word? It is the living Word who infuses the Scripture with Spirit and life.

Clearly understanding that Jesus' life is flowing through you and operating in you is essential for understanding everything else about faith. His life is the underlying reality, the ground from which faith grows.

Jesus taught us that His Spirit-life in us would be superior to His physical presence with us. He said to His disciples, who had grown dependent upon His earthly presence, "'But I tell you the truth: It is *for your good* that I am going away. Unless I go away, the Counselor will not come to you; but if I go, I will send him to you'" (John 16:7). Jesus said that His life indwelling us in Spirit form would be to our benefit. Why? Because from within, Jesus Himself would speak directly into our understanding. We can hear Him more clearly than the disciples could hear Him when He was on earth in physical form. We can hear with understanding. "Though I have been speaking figuratively, a time is coming when I will no longer use this kind of language but will tell you plainly about my Father" (John 16:25). You live in the time when Jesus promised He would "tell you plainly about [His] Father."

We can hear His *rhema*, His present-tense speaking, all the time. He never leaves us. This form of hearing—hearing from within, Spirit-voice to spirit-ears—is superior to hearing with our earth-ears. Spirit-hearing is more reliable than earth-hearing. Jesus said it is *for our benefit* that He has made His Spirit-life available and has removed His physical presence.

Depend on His life flowing through you right now. Depend on His Spirit-voice speaking to your understanding. Any understanding about spiritual truth that you acquire comes directly from Him. He may use a tool—a teacher, a writer, a preacher—but that person is a tool, not a source. He is the one and only source of spiritual understanding. Trust Him. He speaks by opening your mind so that you can understand the Scripture (Luke 24:31–32).

The Discipline of the Word

Your faith rests on the Word of God. The Word of God is the cornerstone of faith. Matthew records a parable that Jesus told. It goes like this.

Therefore everyone who hears these words of mine and puts them into practice is like a wise man who built his house on the rock. The rain came down, the streams rose, and the winds blew and beat against that house; yet it did not fall, because it had its foundation on the rock. But everyone who hears these words of mine and does not put them into practice is like a foolish man who built his house on sand. The rain came down, the streams rose, and the winds blew and beat against that house, and it fell with a great crash.

—Matthew 7:24–27

The Hebrew understanding of the word "hear" is to hear and respond. God's Word will always call for a response from you. Either you will say "yes" to it, or you will say "no" to it. You will either take hold of it, or you will push it away. It calls you to obedience because it is the living Word in written form. In *Holiest of All* Andrew Murray explains, "When the perfect heavenly life of the Lord Jesus comes down from heaven into our hearts, it can assume no other form but that which it had in Him—obedience."

Jesus said that the person who responds to His voice has built her life on a firm foundation. Nothing that life throws at her can tear her down. Jesus said that it is His words that form this foundation upon which strong faith can be built.

Jesus calls His words "seeds." In Mark 4:2–8, Jesus tells a parable that uses the earth-picture of a seed to demonstrate the truth about the Word of God. A seed will remain a seed, will produce nothing, until it is placed into a nurturing environment. The environment needed by the Word of God is the human heart or mind. Once the seed is planted, it produces fruit. Once the Word is planted in your mind, it will bear fruit.

This parable goes on to say that some seeds "grew and produced a crop, multiplying thirty, sixty, or even a hundred times" (Mark 4:8).

Ask the Lord for a hundred-fold increase. Ask Him to bring forth a full and running-over crop of wisdom and insight.

Recognize the importance of Scripture to lay a foundation for your faith, and make every opportunity to absorb it. Marinate your mind in it. When you marinate a cut of meat, you submerge the meat in the marinade. The marinade seeps into the meat, infusing the cells of the meat with its own flavor. It tenderizes the meat, breaking down tough sinew, making it palatable. The longer you let it marinate, the more effectively the marinade does its work. Marinate your mind in the Word of God. Keep your thoughts there, letting it do its transforming work.

I wrote a book called *Riches Stored in Secret Places* in which I lay out a suggestion for a 12-week commitment to learning how to marinate your mind in the Word, letting the living Jesus speak it to you. I teach you seven methods for handling the Word of God in such a way that it becomes Spirit and life. What I have discovered is that when you open your life fully to God's Word, letting it speak living truth into your life, you find that you accidentally memorize it. At least, that is how it works for me, and I have heard the same from many readers responding to *Riches Stored in Secret Places*. You memorize it because it has been so fully absorbed into your thinking. In my experience, that has far more benefit than trying to memorize a certain number of verses or memorizing a verse because it is an assignment. When some words from the Scripture jump up and nest in your heart, you will gradually memorize them.

Let me briefly outline the methods I suggest in *Riches Stored in Secret Places*.

Each week you will ask the Spirit to reveal the layers of truth in a passage of Scripture. I will share some thoughts with you about that Scripture, then I will guide you to meditate on it and pray through it.

I am going to teach you the methods God has taught me, but the Holy Spirit will help you develop your own methods. You will be looking at the same Scripture passage each day for a week at a time, but from slightly different angles. You will discover the prism effect: When you look at a passage of Scripture from different angles, you will see the Light being disseminated with different intensities and shadings. You will find that truth emerges from the Spirit and is built into your life line by line and precept by precept. You will find this to be a great adventure because the Holy Spirit will guide you into all truth. You will discover levels of understanding you have never had before....

DAY ONE: Read through the Scripture and devotional thoughts. Go slowly. Any time a thought captures your attention, stop and re-read it. Underline it. Let it soak in.

DAY TWO: Take the Scripture passage apart and look at each piece separately. Write down each phrase. Beside it, write down your own sense of what that phrase is saying to you. Pay particular attention to words like "if...then," "so that," "because," "therefore," "but," "and," and "when." Underline or circle these words and consider how they reveal connections or cause and effect relationships.

During this meditative exercise, listen for the Holy Spirit to prompt you by bringing to mind other Scripture verses or passages that shed more light on any phrase in this passage. Write them down. Next, put the pieces back together. From your meditation, paraphrase the Scripture passage.

While you are doing this meditative exercise, also be aware of any word, phrase, or concept that creates a picture in your mind. God created our brains so that they work by turning words and phrases and thoughts into mental pictures. If I were to say the word "tree," your mind would immediately "see" a tree. God uses that feature of your brain by using visual language in His Word. If a phrase or a concept creates a picture in your mind, sketch it out or describe it. You don't have to be a great artist. These drawings are, once again, to explore truth from different angles and to solidify your thoughts.

DAY THREE: On Day Three, I want to introduce you to what I call my "Jeopardy Method" of meditating. "Jeopardy" is a popular game in which the player, having been given the answer, must supply the question. Look at the Scripture and ask yourself: "What questions does this passage answer?" List the questions and the answers. I usually go phrase by phrase or thought by thought. When you are finished, look back through your list. You will see new angles to the truth.

DAY FOUR: As you have meditated this week, what has God said directly to you? Write down your name, then write what you are hearing God say. For example, I might write down, "Darling Jennifer," or "Beloved Daughter," or "Apple of My Eye," or "Highly Favored One," or any endearment I hear Him use toward me. Then I would write out His personal Word to me from my meditations. Take time on this morning to enjoy His passionate, tender love for you. Even when His word to you is a word of correction or reproof, it is loving and gentle.

DAY FIVE: Write your honest, heart-felt response to God. In your private time with Him, learn to use terms of endearment. Call Him "Daddy," like Jesus did. Call Him "My Greatest Love," "Beloved," or "My Life." Learn to be lovingly intimate and at ease with Him.

DAY SIX: Based on your meditations this week, what assurances or promises has God made you in His Word? Write them down. Pray these promises as the Holy Spirit applies them to people or situations He has assigned to you for intercession. Write the name or situation next to the promise. Date it. Think of this exercise as harvesting each promise and praying it into that life or situation. When the Father says in His Word that all of His promises are already "yes" in Christ, that causes me to picture a field of ripe and ready grain. The grain is ready to harvest. When we pray based on God's promises, we are harvesting those promises. You do not have to watch to see if God will fulfill His Word. Instead, watch to see how God is fulfilling His Word.

DAY SEVEN: Based on your listening to God, write out faith-statements for your life. This provides you with the basis for praise, worship, and adoration. Spend your contemplative time today praising and worshiping God the Father, God the Son, and God the Spirit. Inwardly, privately, worship with abandon.

Sing to Him. Applaud Him. Kiss His hands. Anoint His feet. Shout "Hosanna!" Bow before Him. Worship Him with abandon.
With these methods, you will be depositing His Word in your mind so that He can continually make withdrawals from it. As you continue to marinate your life in His truth, the Spirit will make connections between passages. You will notice a thread of truth running through the Word. Suddenly, at an unexpected moment, God will shine a searchlight on a truth from a Scripture you thought you had already mined. You will see something clearly that you had not noticed or put together before. It will be so plain that you will wonder how it escaped you. The key is to keep depositing the Word.

—Jennifer Kennedy Dean, *Riches Stored in Secret Places*

Read, study, memorize, meditate. Sing the Word. Think on it as you fall asleep at night and let it greet you first thing when you wake up. Read books that point you to the Word. Listen to teaching that gives sound instruction in the Word. Talk about it with fellow believers. Hang Scripture art on your walls.

I think technology has opened new ways to explore Scripture and feed on it continually. Let me tell you about two things I do. There are many Bible computer programs available. When I want to focus on a book or a section of Scripture, I copy and paste that section into a word processing program. Then I double-space it and leave a wide margin on the right-hand side of the page. Often, I will copy the section from several different translations. Then I print it, three-hole-punch it, and put it in a notebook. Now I can write all over it, circle things, make notes in the margins, put sticky notes on it, draw pictures, or whatever I want to do.

Another thing I do is read into a digital recorder the book or section of Scripture I am focusing on. I can read it with the emphasis and inflection I want it to have. Then I just listen to it as I'm falling asleep and let it play while I sleep. I'm convinced that your dreaming mind is influenced by things you are hearing while you sleep. I have a very scientific basis for this. One night I fell asleep with the television on. I dreamed a detailed dream, but woven throughout it was a recurring theme. No matter what else the actors in my dream were doing, they were all getting hair implants. I woke up to find that there was an infomercial for hair implants on the television. I thought, "Well, if information about hair implants can insert itself into my dreaming mind, then certainly the Word of God can."

Scripture says the same thing. "I will bless the Lord who has counseled me; Indeed, my mind instructs me in the night" (Psalm 16:7 NASB). The Lord counsels me—teaches, advises, guides me—by His Word. Then my mind continues to receive that instruction even during the night. God has created your brain so that this is possible. When you go to sleep, the cognitive portion of your mind goes into a neutral state and the subconscious part of your brain is predominant. Your subconscious mind does not have to follow all the many rules that your conscious mind does, so it can think in fresh and creative ways. All night long, your mind is sorting out new information and comparing it to old information. When you are in your deepest sleep state, brain scans show that your brain is every bit as active as when you are wide awake. Researchers say that when you are learning new information, you have to sleep on it before your brain can fully assimilate it.

Often people tell me that they feel guilty because they fall asleep at night while they are praying. I say, "Have you ever heard of prayer sleeping?" You've heard of prayerwalking, right? Well, now you've heard of prayer sleeping. Go to sleep praying, and you will be praying all through the night. You may wake up during the night with a person on your mind, or a song in your mind, or any number of indications that you have been prayer sleeping. When you wake up in the morning, you will be in a state of prayer. When you go to sleep listening to the Word, you are prayer sleeping. The Word of God is actively working in you and speaking to you all through the night, creating Spirit-formed prayer.

Soak your life in the Word. It is building a firm foundation for your faith.

Questions for Discussion

1. What are some practical ways that you can marinate your mind in God's Word?

2. How does it change your approach to the Scripture when you know it is alive and active and that the Holy Spirit is speaking it into your life?

3. What is the Spirit saying to you from the written Word right now that is calling for a response from you?

Chapter Seven

THE HEAVENS AND THE EARTH

By faith we understand that the universe was formed at God's command,
so that what is seen was not made out of what was visible.

—Hebrews 11:3

Focus first on this phrase: "what is seen was not made out of what was visible." The Greek word for "what is seen" is a word that most often means, "to see with the bodily eye." So this means physical seeing or the things that your physical eyes can see. "Visible" is the translation of another Greek word that also refers to the physical sense of seeing. But the things you can see were not made out of things you can see. Then what were they made of? What is the universe made out of?

"By faith we understand that the universe was formed at God's command." Those things which you can see—the universe—were made out of the word (*rhema* in Greek) of God. Remember the Hebrew word used in the creation account? (*'amar*) It means "to say" and comes from a root meaning "to make visible." It is probably the Hebrew word that the Greek is interpreting here. The physical, material creation was made out of God's word. God's word is the substance of which earth is made. "By the word of the Lord were the heavens made, their starry host by the breath of his mouth" (Psalm 33:6).

Imagine that I am standing in front of you with a lump of clay in my hand. Now imagine that I take that lump of clay and form it into a ball. If I hold this clay ball up in front of you and ask, "What am I holding?" you might well answer, "You're holding a ball."

Suppose I press further and I say, "But what is the ball made out of?" You'll say, "The ball is made out of clay."

"Well, then," I'll conclude, "What I'm holding is *clay* in the shape of a ball."

If the earth is made out of God's word, then isn't the earth really God's word in earth-form? "The heavens declare the glory of God; the skies proclaim the work of his hands. Day after day they pour forth speech; night after night they display knowledge. There is no speech or language where their voice is not heard. Their voice goes out into all the earth, their words to the ends of the world" (Psalm 19:1–4). To put it simply, creation is always talking about God.

Romans 1:20 says, "Since the creation of the world God's invisible qualities—his eternal power and divine nature—have been clearly seen, being understood from what has been made." Look carefully at what Paul said. The qualities of God that you cannot observe directly by using your physical senses can be observed in His creation.

Creation is God's *rhema*. It declares Him. It explains Him. It points to Him. It reveals Him.

Invisible Becomes Visible

This is how it has been from the beginning. When God speaks, that which is invisible takes on earthly substance. That which is in the spiritual realm moves into the earthly realm. When God created the earth, He put eternal reality into a physical construct. He packaged spiritual truth in atoms and molecules. He painted pictures and molded sculptures of eternity.

When God created the elements of earth, each element pictured an eternal reality. Most of the words in the Greek and in the Hebrew and

Aramaic that describe the creating process are words that foundation-ally mean "to order, to arrange, to fit one piece with another." There is nothing random or impulsive about creation. It is a detailed, careful arrangement and description of spiritual reality. When God created light, for example, He was creating a symbol of an eternal principle. Light, as earth knows it, exists because in eternity there is light. When God gave Moses the instructions for building the tabernacle, He told Moses to be sure to follow the instructions to the last detail because he was making a model of a reality that existed in the heavenly realms. I believe that is what every atom of earth is—a model of a reality that exists in the eternal realm.

What was the reason that God worked this way? So that we would always understand, by faith, that what is invisible and in the spiritual realm will be made visible in the earthly realm by the Word of God. He "calls things that are not as though they were" (Romans 4:17). He calls out loud to things that are invisible and commands them to be visible. He calls out loud to things in the spiritual realm and they move into the material realm.

Created and Sustained

Describing Jesus, Paul writes, "sustaining all things by his powerful word" (Hebrews 1:3*a*). What holds everything together? What glues atom to atom and cell to cell? The dynamic, explosive power (*dunamis*) of Jesus' *rhema*. You know the word *rhema* by now. If Jesus were not speaking out every moment, then the earth and all creation would fly apart. "All things were created by him and for him. He is before all things, and in him *all things hold together*" (Colossians 1:16*b*–17).

The very structure of the universe repeats this fact over and over, calling it out to every corner of creation. In the material creation, what is the force that holds all matter together? (Matter is anything that takes up space and has weight.) What is the force that holds the solar system together and forces it into its perfect rotation? The answer is gravity.

Gravity is the ultimate mystery. Let me quote from an article in *Discover* magazine: "All the ordinary matter we can find accounts for only about 4 percent of the universe. We know this by calculating how much mass would be needed to hold galaxies together and cause them to move about the way they do when they gather in large clusters. Another way to weigh the unseen matter is to look at how gravity bends the light from distant objects. Every measure tells astronomers that most of the universe is invisible" (Eric Haseltine, "The Eleven Greatest Unanswered Questions of Physics," *Discover*, February 2002).

Here is the mystery. Gravity is created by mass. The heavier the mass, the stronger gravitational force it creates. When scientists add up all the mass in the universe—the weight of all the planets and suns and moons and stars and little floating specs like neutrinos—the universe does not weigh enough to account for all the gravity that exists and holds it together. So what holds the universe together? The voice of Jesus calling life and order into the universe.

> *What holds the universe together? The voice of Jesus calling life and order into the universe.*

In another article from *Discover* magazine, Robert Kunzig wrote an article called "The Glue That Holds the World Together." Here is his opening paragraph: "You do not know what stuff is, you who hold it in your hands. Atoms? Yes, stuff is made of atoms. And every atom is a nucleus orbited by electrons. Every nucleus is built of protons. Every proton is—but there you reach the end of the line. Inside the proton lies the deep, unsettling truth: Stuff is made of nothing, or almost nothing, held together by glue, lots of glue" (*Discover*, July 2000).

The "glue" to which Kunzig refers in this article is subatomic particles called "gluons," and they hold neutrinos together, which hold atoms together. When you reduce it all down, all matter is made of invisible energy or power.

Some years ago, scientists believed that matter was solid and static.

That was before the discovery of the true structure of the atom. Actually, matter is made of up billions and billions of tiny, microscopic solar systems called atoms. An atom is in constant motion. In each atom, electrons orbit around a nucleus. The nucleus is made up of protons and neutrons strongly bound together. When the atom is split, the incredible force that binds the protons and neutrons together is released and we have atomic energy. So, when matter is reduced to its smallest element, particles orbiting inside an atom, and that atom is split, what remains? Pure energy—power. What is the power that holds the atom's nucleus together—the power that is released when it is split? What is the power that binds atom to atom? No one knows. But the Scripture says that Jesus holds the universe together with His powerful Word.

All matter is being held together by the force of subatomic (smaller than an atom) particles that are in continual high-speed motion. The air around you is not empty. It, too, is made up of atoms in motion. When sounds are made—when you speak, for example—the sound of your voice causes a physical change in the air molecules. It sets up a sound wave. By means of a sound wave, the energy introduced into the air molecules creates a wave effect in the air molecules around them, and the effect moves outward progressively in a wave. So, see if you agree with me that God's creation tells this story: God spoke and by His act of speaking, an incomprehensible power set all matter into place, infusing it with life and order. He continues to speak, and the eternal sound waves of His voice keep the tiniest particles of matter moving in their rhythms, holding His creation together.

Scientists who study physics and the structures that make up the universe continue to be astounded as each discovery leads them back to the reality that matter, at its core, is some invisible force. Robert Kunzig, in the *Discover* article quoted earlier called "The Glue That Holds the World Together," ends his article with a quote from respected scientist Frank Wilczek: "If you really study the equations, it gets almost mystical."

Scientists agree that the amount of matter on the earth never changes. Matter changes forms. Water, for example, may transform into gas. A mountain may be eroded by a river, but the mountain's mass has now taken up residence in the water. Everything that God originally spoke into being still exists. His word stands firm and immoveable. No one can subtract from it or add to it.

Invisible Matter

Most of the universe is invisible. So say those who study it closely—those who put it under powerful microscopes and examine it from every vantage point. Most of creation is invisible. They refer to "dark matter" and "dark energy," by which they mean energy and substance that are hidden from view. They must exist, but we just can't see them.

Neutrinos are an example. "Neutrinos, unseen and beyond counting, fill the universe. People call them ghostly, but ghosts aren't real. Neutrinos are real." No one has ever seen one, but the effects they produce prove their existence. Stranger still, "it seems that a given neutrino does not have one stable mass or one stable identity. Instead, as it flies along, it oscillates from one identity—what physicists call a flavor, which means a way of interacting with other particles—to another." Neutrinos, which no one has ever seen, are so numerous that "if they have even a tiny mass, they outweigh all the stars and galaxies, all the visible matter in the universe. They might make up as much as one fifth of the dark matter that physicists and astrophysicists have been seeking so assiduously" (Robert Kunzig, "The Unbearably Unstoppable Neutrino," *Discover*, August 2001).

Now think about this. The most fact-based, pragmatic, proof-demanding physicists say that most of the universe is invisible. They don't claim that it doesn't exist, just that it is invisible. So if you look at the air and it looks empty, it's not. That is an illusion. In fact, there is no such thing as "emptiness."

Now—fair warning—here comes one of my adventurous thoughts

I warned you about, just a "what if." What if the spiritual realm, which we might tend to think of as "a galaxy far, far away," to borrow a phrase from *Star Wars*, is really not far, far away? What if it is really all around you? What if all that dark energy and dark mass is really the spiritual realm operating in direct interaction with the material realm? Jesus said, "Repent, for the kingdom of heaven is near" (Matthew 4:17b), "Repent"—change your mind. But more than just change your opinion, it means think differently. It means reorient your mind. Set it differently. Tune your thoughts to a different dimension. Why? Because the kingdom of heaven is "near," or as the King James Version says, "at hand." The Greek word means that it is squeezing you, pressing in on you. At hand—reach out your hand and there it is. I have often thought about how easily Jesus moved back and forth between time and eternity—between material and physical—during the 40 days when He appeared on earth after His resurrection and before His ascension. He was in the spiritual realm, invisible, and the next moment He was in the material realm. I don't think He was traveling back and forth between two widely separated locations, do you? The molecular structure of His body just changed to accommodate one realm or the other. When He is invisible, He is still present.

Now, I know that the kingdom of God is within us, but I think it is of such a composition that it is in us and around us and through us and between us. Neutrinos are constantly traveling through us, in one side and out the other. If neutrinos can be around us and in us and through us, surely so can the kingdom.

Whatever the explanation, the spiritual realm is present and active in our lives. It is not a different location, but a different dimension. It is real and solid and available every moment.

His Powerful Word

Look around you. God's Word is everywhere you look. In Him you live and move and have your being. He is all and is in all. His Word washes over you like waves of the sea. Breathe it in. Taste it. The Word of God lives.

Your faith has a firm foundation.

Questions for Discussion

1. Why can we define the earth as God's word in earth forms?

2. What does it mean for you that you are living in and breathing in the living word of God?

3.What difference does it make to you that the kingdom of God is at hand—there for the taking?

Chapter Eight

SEEING GOD'S WORD

I pray also that the eyes of your heart may be enlightened in order that you may know.

—Ephesians 1:18a

God intends for you to know, understand, and be filled with His will so that you will have confidence in prayer, walking daily in the power of prayer. How will you know the nuances of God's will along with those aspects of His will clearly written in Scripture?

Paul says this: "I pray also that the eyes of your heart may be enlightened in order that you may *know* the hope to which he has called you, the riches of his glorious inheritance in the saints, and his incomparably great power for us who believe" (Ephesians 1:18–19a). God wants to *show* you His will. He wants your inner eyes to receive light so that you will *know*. The Greek word translated "know" in this passage literally means "to see; not the mere act of seeing but the actual perception of some object; to see and understand." This particular Greek word suggests fullness of knowledge, not progressing or growing in knowledge. To know in this sense means to fully understand. God's plan is that we will see the hope, the riches, and the power.

"I see!" You've probably used these words to mean, "I understand fully!" God wants you to see the hope of your calling, the riches available to you, and His incomparably great power for you. Jesus said to

Nicodemus, "'I tell you the truth, no one can see the kingdom of God unless he is born again'" (John 3:3). To state it another way, if a person is born again, he can see the kingdom of God. The person whom the Spirit of God indwells has the spiritual ability to see. Seeing spirit-truth changes one's perception of material facts.

Here's what I mean: Jesus suggested to Nicodemus that the Spirit is like the wind. Once again, Jesus points to an earth-picture to explain a spirit-truth. The wind has no substance. You don't know where it comes from or where it's going. You can't grab hold of it and feel its texture. You only know wind because of its effects.

Suppose, then, that a person decides that he does not believe in the wind. Wind, he decides, is the figment of someone's imagination. No one can prove wind. He prefers to stick to things that can be empirically proven. This person will reach some strange conclusions about what is true. For example, this person will conclude that trees lean over all by themselves sometimes; or that leaves lying quietly on the ground sometimes jump up and twirl through the air. This person will ascribe power where there is no power. He will not understand that the trees and the leaves are responding to a power that is acting on them.

If a person who does not believe in the wind and a person who believes in and understands the wind look at the same scene, they will see two startlingly different truths. The first will see trees bending over; the second will see the wind.

The person who learns to observe with spirit-eyes will look at earth and see spirit. This person will understand that everything he sees on the earth is the effect of spirit. This person will know and understand the whole truth, the reality, and will not be limited to time-bound, earth-bound perceptions and short-sighted vision. This person, seeing the truth, will be free to live in harmony with it, no longer bound to and limited by a caricature of the truth. Jesus said, "If you hold to my teaching, you are really my disciples. Then you will know the truth, and *the truth will set you free*" (John 8:31–32).

See the Kingdom

Jesus uses the language of "seeing" when He explains how He knew God's will while limited to His earth-abilities. He said, "'I tell you the truth, the Son can do nothing by himself; he can do only what he *sees* his Father doing, because whatever the Father does the Son also does. For the Father loves the Son and *shows* him all he does'" (John 5:19–20*a*). Another time He stated, "'I am telling you what I have *seen* in the Father's presence'" (John 8:38*a*). When Jesus makes these statements, He is not talking about what He saw in His pre-existent state when He was with the Father before He came to earth. When Jesus came to earth, He took upon Himself the form of a man. In other words, He limited Himself to living in time and space. He has no access to pre-existent knowledge.

God gives His children spiritual vision. In order to understand how spiritual vision functions, we'll look at physical vision.

What is "vision"? Vision is the ability to see. What I *see* becomes what I *know*. For example, once I see the color red, I know what the color red looks like. Yet I can never know what red is without seeing it. Once I see a person's face, I know what that person looks like. I can never know it without seeing it. Everything I see becomes part of what I know.

What I see gives me direction. I have to see where I'm going in order to get to my destination. I need physical vision to navigate my physical world.

However, I don't see with my eyes. I see with my brain. My eyeballs receive the stimuli, reflected light, which is carried as electrical impulses to my brain. When the electrical impulses reach my occipital lobe, an image registers on my brain. My brain interprets it, decides on the proper response, stamps it into my memory, and processes it into everything else that I know. "Seeing" is a finished work when my brain has developed a picture and has given it what we call "meaning."

The brain's ability to see can be activated by the imagination or the memory. Your brain can picture a familiar scene or can create a scene out of random information stored in your memory bank. Your brain does not need your eyes in order to create a picture once the picture has initially been seen. It's all in the brain. "Seeing" is when a picture is imprinted on your brain so that it becomes part of what you know.

If I said your spouse's name, or your child's name, or your best friend from childhood's name, you could immediately "see" his or her face. If I said, "Think about sitting at your kitchen table with a cup of coffee," you could "see" the table and the coffee cup. You see with your brain.

Vision differs from the other physical senses. To use any of the other senses, you need only two things: the stimulus and the ability to receive the stimulus. In other words, to hear, you need something to hear and the ability to hear it; to taste, you need something to taste and the ability to taste it. Each sense works this way—except the sense of sight. Sight requires the presence of a third element. In order to see, you need *something to see, the ability to see it,* and *LIGHT*.

Vision occurs when your eyes receive the light reflected off an object and send the image to your brain. Without the presence of light, vision cannot occur.

Spiritual vision works the same way. Spiritual vision occurs when God creates a picture within your mind—on your brain—of spiritual realities. In physical vision, the impetus for sight is light bouncing off physical objects. In spiritual vision, the impetus for sight is light reflected off spiritual realities. Vision cannot occur without a light source. The light source for spiritual vision is Jesus. Recall that God created light for the earth because light existed in the eternal realms. The light we know on earth is pointing us to the light that has always been.

The Jesus-light illuminates kingdom realities. They register on my understanding and become part of what I know. Remember Paul's prayer? "I pray that the eyes of your heart will be enlightened so that you will *know*" (Ephesians 1:18).

Solid, true, authentic kingdom realities are within you. When you were born into the kingdom of God, the kingdom of God was born into you. Kingdom realities are within you and "the true light that gives light to every man" (John 1:9), Jesus, is causing you to "see" them. They are imprinted on your brain. You understand them.

How will you know the hope to which He has called you? How will you know His riches which He has invested in you? How will you know His incomparably great power that is working for you and in you? He will give you light. He will enlighten the eyes of your heart. Then you will know. You will see and fully perceive.

Through the steady discipline of prayer, spiritual vision is sharpened. The more we live in His presence, the more opportunity He has to enhance our ability to see and bring into sharper focus what we already see. Spiritual vision is faith. "Now faith is being sure of what we hope for and certain of what we do not see" (Hebrews 11:1).

Spiritual Vision Surpasses Physical Vision

The person with clear spiritual vision will recognize dimensions of reality that are invisible to the physical senses. In the second chapter of Luke we are introduced to two such people.

"Now there was a man in Jerusalem called Simeon, who was righteous and devout. He was waiting for the consolation of Israel, and the Holy Spirit was upon him. It had been revealed to him by the Holy Spirit that he would not die before he had seen the Lord's Christ" (Luke 2:25–26). What have we learned about Simeon so far? We know that he has no distinctive titles and holds no position of leadership. He is described merely as a man in Jerusalem. We know that the Holy Spirit was upon him. In other words, he was especially attuned to the moving of the Spirit and his life was open and available for the Spirit's leadings. We know that God had placed into Simeon's life a vision—a clear mental picture of a future event. The vision is a promise from God. The Spirit had revealed to Simeon that he would not die until he had seen the Messiah.

In verses 27 through 30 we read, "Moved by the Spirit, he went into the temple courts. When the parents brought in the child Jesus to do for him what the custom of the law required, Simeon took him in his arms and praised God, saying: 'Sovereign Lord, as you have promised, you now dismiss your servant in peace. For my eyes have seen your salvation'" (Luke 2:27–30). Now we see that Simeon, moving in the flow of the Spirit, went to the temple where he saw Mary and Joseph bringing the infant Jesus "to do for him what the custom of the law required." Do you see what that phrase implies? Mary and Joseph were doing something ordinary—something every Jewish family did. Probably other families were doing the same thing on the same day. Many people that day looked at Mary and Joseph and the infant Jesus. Yet when Simeon looked at this ordinary, everyday scene, he saw what no one else saw. He saw the Messiah when everybody else saw a mother and a father and a baby. Others saw the appearance. Simeon saw the Truth.

Next we meet a woman named Anna. In Luke 2:36–38, we learn that Anna was a prophetess. She was especially called and gifted by God to discern His activity in the world. She had spent most of her life worshiping, fasting, and praying. In prayer, she had developed an extreme sensitivity to the moving of the Spirit. Like Simeon, when she looked at the family from Nazareth, she recognized the Messiah, the Promise of God.

Nothing in the material realm identified Jesus as God's Promised One. Only those who had spiritual vision recognized Him. Those who knew the Scriptures and the Law best, the religious leaders of the day, did not recognize the Truth when He stood in front of them. Jesus said they were "blind guides." Their spiritual eyes were darkened, and they did not see the Spirit. Their understanding was limited to things they could perceive with their physical senses.

You have a layer of spiritual senses that your bodily senses represent. You will always have a choice. You can look at situations from the limitations of your earthly perceptions, or you can look with the eyes of spirit. You can see the kingdom.

Giants or Grasshoppers

When you walk in faith, you will train your eyes to see the reality of the spiritual realm rather than the facts as your senses perceive them. With practice, this will become your natural way of seeing things. My friend Joanne, whose daughter is a photographer, had this thought. Have you ever looked at the negative of a photograph? It is exactly the opposite of the photograph. Where the photograph is light, the negative is dark. Where the photograph is dark, the negative is light. Hold the negative up to the light and the scene changes. What appeared to be dark is really light. The true picture emerges. Let Him show you that every negative, when held up to the light, becomes a positive. Practice until your automatic response to any fearful, critical, negative thought is faith. *Learn* to see the positive. It will make all the difference.

God promised the nation of Israel a land flowing with milk and honey, a land that produced lush fruit and abundant grain. The land was called Canaan. As the Israelites reached the boundaries of Canaan after leaving Egypt, the Lord instructed Moses to send out a group of men to explore the land and bring back a report. It interests me that 12 men looked at the same scene, but they viewed it differently. All twelve spies actually brought back the same report. In essence, all of them agreed on the facts as follows: "The land is just exactly as God said it would be. It flows with milk and honey. Its fruit is large and its grain is lush. And there are giants in the land." They all agreed on the facts, but they interpreted the facts differently.

Ten of the men saw the negative: "We went into the land to which you sent us, and it does flow with milk and honey! Here is its fruit. But the people who live there are powerful, and the cities are fortified and very large....The land we explored devours those living in it. All the people we saw there are of great size....We seemed like grasshoppers in our own eyes, and we looked the same to them" (Numbers 13:27–28; 32–33).

Two of the men, Joshua and Caleb, had a different view. "The land we passed through and explored is exceedingly good. If the LORD is pleased with us, he will lead us into that land, a land flowing with milk and honey, and will give it to us. Only do not rebel against the LORD. And do not be afraid of the people of the land, because we will swallow them up. Their protection is gone, but the LORD is with us. Do not be afraid of them" (Numbers 14:7–9).

The ten said, "We are grasshoppers in the eyes of our enemies!" Joshua and Caleb said, "Our enemies are grasshoppers in the eyes of the Lord!" The ten said, "They will devour us!" Joshua and Caleb said, "We will swallow them up." The very same facts that caused fear in the ten, instead engaged faith in Caleb and Joshua. Caleb and Joshua saw an opportunity for God to act. They saw a platform for His power. They held the negative up to the light and saw the positive.

Spiritual vision will enable you to see everything in the light of Jesus.

Spiritual Vision Works Two Ways

In Simeon, we can clearly see vision working in two ways. The first way we can see vision working is in Simeon's ability to see the Spirit in an ordinary event. When he looked at earth, he saw Spirit-truth—he saw the wind. He was alert to the Spirit. He expected the promise. Spiritual vision gives the ability to discern between appearance and truth.

Second, God gave him a specific promise upon which Simeon could base his prayers. God showed Simeon through His Spirit that Simeon would see the Messiah before he died. The Scripture says it had been revealed to him. This wording implies that the promise did not come in a sudden one-time encounter but progressively took root in his understanding as he lived in the anointing of the Spirit. The idea grew in him and took on substance until he knew it with certainty. In his own mind, he could see it. It became part of what he knew.

Over and over again we see in the Scripture that God works by first implanting vision. Abraham, Noah, Moses, Gideon, Paul, Jesus...the list goes on. God implants vision. God nurtures vision. God causes vision to become reality on the earth.

God Implants Vision

Vision is Spirit-work. Only God can put promise in you and make it vision. Truth, when it is external, is an idea or a belief. It only becomes vision when it is within you. Like a baby grows inside a woman's body until the time for it to be born onto the earth, vision grows in the spirit of a believer until the time for it to become reality on the earth.

When God brought forth on the earth His ultimate promise, He did so by means of pregnancy and birth. Again, we can see an earth-picture that teaches a spirit-principle. God will impregnate you with vision. Vision is a specific promise from God to you. He takes what He sees for you and develops a picture of it in your mind. It develops gradually, slowly but surely becoming sharp and clear. God puts promises (vision) in us and then births them through us.

I want you to examine two incidents reported in Scripture side by side. One is when the angel announced to Mary that she would give birth to the Messiah. The other is when the Holy Spirit fell on the church at Pentecost. The language is parallel.

> *"You will **be with child** [sullambano] and give birth to a son, and you are to give him the name Jesus."...The angel answered, "The Holy Spirit will **come upon** [eperchomai] you, and the power [dunamis] of the Most High will **overshadow** [episkiazo] you."*
>
> —Luke 1:31, 35a

Let me define the primary words in this passage.

"be with child": *sullambano* "to conceive; to clasp; to take hold"

"come upon": *eperchomai* "to come upon forcefully"

"power": *dunamis* "inherent power; power residing in a thing by virtue of its nature, or which a person or thing exerts and puts forth; explosive power; miraculous power"

"overshadow" *episkiazo* "envelope in a haze; cast a shadow over"

Now look at the second, parallel passage.

> *In a few days you will be **baptized with** [baptizo] the Holy Spirit....But you will **receive** [lambano] **power** [dunamis] when the Holy Spirit **comes on** [eperchomai] you; and you will be my witnesses in Jerusalem, and in all Judea and Samaria, and to the ends of the earth.....All of them were **filled with** [pletho] the Holy Spirit.*
>
> —Acts 1:5, 8; 2:4

The word for "receive," *lambano*, is the root of *sullambano*, "to conceive." The word for "baptized with" means "covered over, overwhelmed; immersed." They were "filled with" the Holy Spirit—this phrase means not only to be filled up, but also to be fulfilled or completed. Do you see the pattern?

MARY	CHURCH
Overshadowed by the Most High	Overwhelmed by the Holy Spirit
Holy Spirit fell upon her	Holy Spirit fell upon them
The power inherent in God was infused into her	The power inherent in God was infused into them
Conceived the Promised One	Received the Promised One (Acts 2:33)
Filled with Holy Spirit	Filled with Holy Spirit

This is God's pattern. This is how He works to put His promises inside you and make them vision.

Pregnant with Promise

Vision will first appear in your life in embryonic form. Vision does not come into your life full-grown. It will need time to gestate. God initiates the vision. You will need to provide the vision with the proper conditions for maturing.

The vision needs a Spirit-womb. Your innermost being available to God's powerful work is the place where the vision grows. Your Spirit-filled life is the environment in which the vision develops.

When a woman finds that she is pregnant, this will often serve as the motivation to change some of her habits. It is an amazing responsibility to be housing another person in her own body. She realizes that everything she physically does is having direct impact on the baby.

As it dawns on you that you are pregnant with promise through the Holy Spirit, you will start to evaluate the way you think and the emotions you foster in your mind and the attitudes you live with. Are you poisoning and stunting the vision? Someone might say to a pregnant woman, "Why aren't you drinking coffee?" She might reply, "I'm with child." Make this your new response to old attitudes: "You can't come in. I'm with promise."

The vision needs nourishment. Feed the vision the Word of God. As you fill your life with God's Word, the vision will grow stronger and healthier. It will take on clearer focus, become more substantive. The natural result of nourishing your spirit will be that the vision God has entrusted to you will mature.

Because the Word of God is living, and is being spoken to you now from the mouth of God, it is not generic or one-size-fits-all. He can speak it right to the promise He has implanted in you. He can apply it directly and specifically. Sometimes you won't even know how the Word is feeding the vision in the moment; you will only recognize it later. But you can count on God's ability to do it.

The vision has developmental stages. Be patient. God always reveals His infinite truth in finite stages. The vision will progressively unfold as you walk in obedience. Consider Abraham. Observe how his vision continued to unfold and develop.

In Genesis 12:1–4, God first implants the vision. "The LORD had said to Abram, 'Leave your country, your people and your father's household and go to the land I will show you. I will make you into a great nation and I will bless you; I will make your name great, and you will be a blessing. I will bless those who bless you, and whoever curses you I will curse; and all peoples on earth will be blessed through you.' So Abraham left, as the LORD had told him."

The vision is vague at best. Abraham is to go to a land that God will show him. God will bless him and make him into a great nation. Abraham knows no more than that. He has no clear picture of the mature plan, just an embryonic vision. But he leaves, as the Lord had told him.

When Abraham reaches a certain place in Canaan, the Lord appears to him. This time He is a little more specific. "To your offspring I will give this land," He says in Genesis 12:7. The vision is taking clearer shape. It moves from "a land I'll show you" to "this land."

In Genesis 13, Abraham has given the vision time and nourishment, and God fleshes it out further. "Lift up your eyes from where you are and look north and south, east and west. All the land that you see I will give to you and your offspring forever. I will make your offspring like the dust of the earth, so that if anyone could count the dust, then your offspring could be counted. Go, walk through the length and breadth of the land, for I am giving it to you" (Genesis 13:14–17). God lays out the boundaries of the land. Furthermore, He expands on His promise to make of Abraham a great nation. He clarifies that the vision is not only qualitative greatness, but numerical greatness.

Abraham has a problem—at least he thinks he does. God has given him the vision of fathering a great nation, but Abraham doesn't even have one son. Abraham expresses his concern. "O Sovereign LORD, what can you give me since I remain childless and the one who will inherit my estate is Eliezer of Damascus? ...You have given me no children; so a servant in my household will be my heir'" (Genesis 15:2–3). Notice how Abraham states his analysis. He says, "You *have given* me no children...a servant *will be* my heir." Abraham thinks it's too late. He sees only one way for God to bring the vision about: He'll have to use Abraham's servant, Eliezer of Damascus. In response, God gives Abraham more detail of the vision, a detail He had not yet stated. "This man will not be your heir, but a son coming from your own body will be your heir" (Genesis 15:4*b*). The vision continues to take on clearer form.

Be patient. God always reveals His infinite truth in finite stages.

In Genesis 15:13–16, God fills in more details. For the first time He tells Abraham that his descendants will be strangers in a country that will enslave them for 400 years, but afterward they will come out with great possessions. In the fourth generation, God says, Abraham's descendants will return to the Promised Land. Then, in verse 18, God adds more specifics. He gives clearer boundaries of the land of the vision. "To your descendants I give this land, from the river of Egypt to the great river, the Euphrates—the land of the Kenites, Kenizzites, Kadmonites, Hittites, Perizzites, Rephaites, Amorites, Canaanites, Girgashites and Jebusites" (Genesis 15:18–21). The vision has progressed from "the land I'll show you," to "this land" to the detailed description above. This is progressive vision. Each step of obedience opens up new dimensions, new understandings. One step makes the next step clear. Step by step, following the voice that grows the vision.

Finally, God appears to Abraham when he is 99 years old. In the physical realm, Abraham still has no heir. Yet God says, "No longer will you be called Abram; your name will be Abraham, for I have made you a father of many nations" (Genesis 17:5). Do you see what God said? "I *have made you* a father of many nations." Before that, God had said "I *will make you* a father of many nations." In the spiritual realm, the work is done. The only thing left is for spiritual truth to be manifested in the material realm. In verses 6 through 14, God sets forth the terms of the covenant. He gives Abraham a sign of the covenant in the flesh—circumcision. He tells Abraham clearly that not only will the heir come from his own body, but from the body of his wife Sarah. He says, "But my covenant I will establish with Isaac, whom Sarah will bear to you this time next year" (Genesis 17:21). Now the vision is full-term. It is ready to be born on the earth.

The vision has a due date. "For the vision is yet for the appointed time; It hastens toward the goal and it will not fail. Though it tarries, wait for it; For it will certainly come, it will not delay" (Habakkuk 2:3 NASB).

The vision is for an appointed time. God implanted it in your life at exactly the right time and He will bring it about at exactly the right time. My tendency is to try to induce labor as soon as the vision enters my life. I'm inclined to be impatient. It always looks like the right time to me. God is teaching me to wait for the due date. When the vision has reached the right developmental stage, nothing can hold it back. Until that time, nothing can bring it forth. My advice is this: Don't push before it's time.

The vision is God's, not yours. You are only hosting the vision. He has placed His vision into your imagination, creativity, understanding, and desires. *He* will bring about *His* vision. "Surely, as I have planned, so it will be, and as I have purposed, so it will stand" (Isaiah 14:24).

Birthing the vision will involve labor pains. Count on it. The closer the moment of birth, the harder and faster the pains come. The time comes when you have to bear down with all your might. But not until your Birthing Coach says so.

Seeing His Voice

Rabbi Abraham Isaac Kook, the first Chief Rabbi of the State of Israel (he was appointed before it reached statehood), writes some captivating thoughts on the odd Hebrew wording of Exodus 20:18. It follows the giving of the Ten Commandments. The English translations have cleaned it up so that it sounds more plausible. The closest translation seems to be the King James Version, which says, "And all the people saw the thunderings, and the lightnings, the noise of the trumpet, and the mountain smoking: and when the people saw it, they removed and stood afar off" (Exodus 20:18 KJV). In the Hebrew it specifically says, "And all the people *saw* the sounds." Here is what Rav Kook says about it:

> The Midrash calls our attention to an amazing aspect of the Sinaitic revelation: the Jewish people were able to see what is normally only heard. What does this mean?
>
> At their source, sound and sight are united. Only in our limited, physical world, in this "*alma deperuda*" (world of separation), are these phenomena disconnected and detached. It is similar to our perception of lightning and thunder, which become increasingly separated from one another as the observer is more distanced from the source.
>
> If we are bound to the present, and can view the universe only through the temporal, material framework, then we will always perceive this divide between sight and sound. The prophetic vision at Mount Sinai, however, granted the people the unique perspective of one standing near the source of Creation. At that level, they witnessed the underlying unity of the universe. They were capable of seeing sounds and hearing sights. God's revelation at Sinai was registered by all their senses simultaneously, as a single, undivided perception.

In this statement in Exodus 20:18, the word translated "thunderings"—"the people saw the *thunderings*"—is the word for "voice." It is the same word used in the opening chapters of Genesis 3:8 and Genesis 3:10 for God's voice when he spoke to Adam and Eve. So you could as easily say, "All the people saw the voice."

We are closer to His voice than the Israelites at Sinai were. He is inside of us. His word is in our hearts. He is not speaking to us from a mountain, but from inside—closer than close. You are so close to His voice that you can "see" it.

Remember that to see, you need light. The light in the kingdom is Jesus. Paul writes that the light is in "the face of Christ" (2 Corinthians 4:6). God gives us the light of His glory in the face of Jesus.

An emerging science is the study of facial communication, or what you might call "seeing the voice." Studies done on infants 18 to 20 weeks old show that, even at a prelinguistic age, they read facial expressions to understand speech. A thought or emotion registers on the face before it is spoken. The face registers the true emotion, even if the words are meant to mask the emotion. A highly specific science of mapping the facial muscles called Facial Action Coding System is a method by which you can read a person's face and know his thoughts. Even though a person can learn to quickly rearrange his face to mask emotion, the true emotion always registers on the face, even if only fleetingly. "When we experience a basic emotion, a corresponding message is automatically sent to the muscles of the face. That message may linger just a fraction of a second, or be detectable only if you attached electrical sensors to the face, but it's always there" (Malcolm Gladwell, "The Naked Face," *The New Yorker*, August 2002).

Keep your eyes fixed on Jesus' face. You will see His voice.

Recognizing Vision

When God puts His promises in you, you will know it. You'll find that it is woven into your spiritual DNA. You can't get rid of it. You may become discouraged. You may decide one day not to believe it any-more. But you wake up the next day, and you believe it again in spite of yourself. As the vision develops, you can see how God has always been moving you toward the vision. The abilities and interests He has given you, the advantages and the disadvantages, the circumstances—both good and bad—all have been shaping the vision and preparing for its birth.

In the process of developing the vision, God will have to take you through times and bring you to crisis points where you will recognize that you have some of your own flesh wrapped around the promise. God has to circumcise all your flesh from His vision. We'll look at that in detail in the last section of this book, "Faith: The Finish." But until we get there, be aware that it is always God's work in your life when you encounter faith challenges. His work is progressing the vision, even when it is painful.

The Purpose of Spiritual Vision

Why does God do His work through vision? Why engage humans before the fact? Why not just let His work show up on earth unannounced? God says, "See, the former things have taken place, and new things I declare; before they spring into being I announce them to you" (Isaiah 42:9). He announces His intentions into our desires or understanding, and He then brings His intentions into being in response to our prayers. Why?

In Isaiah 48:3–5 we read, "I foretold the former things long ago, my mouth announced them and I made them known; then suddenly I acted, and they came to pass. For I knew how stubborn you were; the sinews of your neck were iron, your forehead was bronze. Therefore I told you these things long ago; before they happened I announced them to you so that you could not say, 'My idols did them; my wooden image and metal god ordained them.'" In other words, God will announce His plans before He brings them into being so that we will recognize His work and will not attribute His power to anyone or anything else.

Jesus said, "I have told you now before it happens, so that when it docs happen you will believe" (John 14:29). When you see the picture inside you take shape on the earth, you will recognize the work of the One who has the power to do what He has promised (Romans 4:21).

God gives impossible vision. If it were possible, it would be an assignment or a project—but it is vision. When vision takes shape on the earth, there will be no doubt about whose vision it is. God will implant vision in you that only He can bring into being. "But we have this treasure in jars of clay to show that this all-surpassing power is from God and not from us" (2 Corinthians 4:7).

If you have scaled back or watered down God's vision, you are not "[taking] hold of that for which Christ Jesus took hold of [you]" (Philippians 3:12*b*). God will not bring about a diluted form of His vision. You may bring about a diluted form of His vision, but He will not. If what you are envisioning about a situation negates or underestimates the power of God, you are not praying the vision, not claiming the promise. You are limiting God by expecting of Him only what you can imagine.

What do you see in the presence of your Father?

Mini-Vision

As you consider this concept, realize that the whole Bible sets this process out as the pattern God established. I believe that there is an overall vision and call for your life, but also "mini-visions" along the way. I believe that in every circumstance He works in this pattern, sometimes more obviously so than others.

So, for example, your marriage is struggling. What do you see in your Father's presence? Your child has strayed from his relationship with the Lord. What do you see in your Father's presence? Whatever you are facing, what do you see in your Father's presence?

A Warning

Let me add a warning and a clarification here. I don't want you to confuse what I'm saying with some of the concepts of visualizing or imaging so prevalent in New Age religions, or with some of the variations on that thinking that have even made their way into the church. The most effective lies are those that are close to the truth.

New Age concepts say that by visualizing or imaging what you want, you can make it happen. In this thought, the vision originates with you and you, by deliberately and consistently imaging what you desire, create that reality. This is NOT what Scripture teaches about how God implants His vision.

A variation on that lie sometimes shows up in the church. Again, the distorted version of the truth puts the emphasis on your flesh. The thinking goes that by envisioning what you want God to do, you will cause God to do it and you will create the "energy" or the "power" to bring it to pass. This is NOT what Scripture teaches about how God implants His vision, either.

Be careful and do not blur the crisp edges of the truth. God gives you the mental picture of His reality—the reality that exists in the heavenly realms and is available to be manifested in the earth. The picture He gives you is so that you can have confidence when things seem discouraging. It is also so that when He creates on the earth the reality He has already shown you, you will recognize His hand at work.

The Firm Foundation

Your faith rests on what God has spoken.

> *Against all hope, Abraham in hope believed and so became the father of many nations, **just as it had been said to him**, "So shall your offspring be." Without weakening in his faith, he faced the fact that his body was as good as dead—since he was about a*

hundred years old—and that Sarah's womb was also dead. Yet he
did not waver through unbelief **regarding the promise of God,**
but was strengthened in his faith and gave glory to God, being
fully persuaded that God had power to do **what He had prom-**
ised. *This is why "it was credited to him as righteousness." The*
words "it was credited to him" were written not for him alone,
but also for us, to whom God will credit righteousness—for us
who believe in him who raised Jesus our Lord from the dead.

—Romans 4:18–24

What did Abraham believe? He believed what had been said to him.
Where was his faith rooted? Paul says that Abraham did not waver
through unbelief regarding the things that God had promised him.
What was Abraham fully persuaded about? That God would do what
He promised to do. Paul then says that this is how God works in the
lives of all of us who believe in Him.

Your faith does not rest on your best ideas, or someone else's pre-
sumptions, or your own perceptions, but on the Word of God, delivered to you in the most personal way possible—implanted in you as
vision.

Questions for Discussion

1. Why does God implant vision in His people?

2. Why does spiritual vision surpass physical vision?

3. Do you recognize vision in your own life?

4. Do you see some particular areas of your life at which the enemy has designed elaborate attacks? Where he comes at you again and again? Might that give you a clue about the vision with which God has impregnated you? Satan would like to destroy it.

Section Three

FAITH:
The Function

Chapter Nine

THE MIDWIFE OF VISION

The promise comes by faith.

—Romans 4:16

How does vision become reality on the earth? How does the picture God has placed within you take shape in the material realm?

"The promise *(vision)* comes *(is translated into reality)* by faith" (Romans 4:16). Faith is the midwife of vision. Examine this statement that Paul made in the Book of Romans:

"The promise comes…"

Comes from where to where? From heaven to earth.

"The promise comes…"

How? What is the avenue that brings the promise from heaven to earth?

"The promise comes by faith."

Faith brings the promise out of heaven and makes it reality on the earth.

When God puts promise in you, faith is the process by which that promise is realized in the circumstances of earth. The promise comes by faith.

What gave life to the promise? The voice of God did. The voice of God that framed the worlds in the beginning is the same voice that frames your world by means of His promises.

Recall the Scripture portions we examined to see the process of being impregnated with promise. God overshadowed Mary and spoke the Word into her womb. Mary conceived. The word means "to take hold of." "And Mary said, 'Behold, the bondslave of the Lord; may it be done to me according to your word'" (Luke 1:38a NASB). Mary received the Word of God. She let it take up residence in her. She let it abide in her (John 15:7) and dwell in her richly (Colossians 3:16).

When the Israelites left Egypt, they left with a promise. God had a land ready for them to inhabit. The generation that left Egypt never entered the Promised Land. Why? The writer of Hebrews explains: "For we also have had the gospel preached to us, just as they did; but the message they heard was of no value to them, because those who heard did not *combine it with faith*" (Hebrews 4:2). Even though they were told about the good news of God's provision for them, it did them no good. For them, there might as well not have been a Promised Land. They lived as if no Promised Land existed. They did not mix the Word of God with faith. The word translated "combine" is a word that means "to unite one thing with another; to cause several parts to combine into an organic structure." For example, consider the difference between a mixture and a solution. In a mixture, several elements are put together, but each retains its original form and can be separated out again. Fruit salad is a mixture. In a solution, the molecules of the elements combine to make an entirely new substance. When salt and water are united, their molecules combine. The salt is dissolved in the water. A whole new substance with a whole new molecular structure results. That is the sense of the Greek word *sugkerannumi*, translated "combine."

Just as in physical conception where the father's sperm must unite with the mother's egg, when God speaks promise into your Spirit-womb, it has to be combined with faith in order for conception to occur. Just as the new life that begins in that moment of physical conception must attach itself to the mother's womb, the vision that is conceived must find a foothold and take root in your mind. It must adhere to your innermost being and be immoveable and steadfast.

So now we wrestle with that fundamental question, what is faith? How does faith function?

Faith Works

It makes sense to me that if you observe how something functions, you then discover its definition. So, by observing faith in operation, I reach the conclusion that faith's central definition—its root definition—is "obedience to the present-tense voice of the Lord."

> This sentence (Hebrews 11:3) is the thesis statement for this whole treatise on faith. From this statement, the writer begins to document his case. Faith, he is saying, is when the invisible power of God's Word—that is His *rhema*, His present-tense word—produces a visible effect on the earth.
>
> Now read through verses 4–40. How does the Scripture define faith?
>
> 1. *"By faith Abel offered..."* (verse 4).
> 2. *"By faith Noah...built..."* (verse 7).
> 3. *"By faith Abraham...obeyed and went"* (verse 8).
> 4. *"By faith Abraham...offered Isaac..."* (verse 17).
> 5. *"By faith Isaac blessed..."* (verse 20).
>
> On and on it goes. These people who are held up as examples of faith were commended for what they did—not felt—in response to God's voice. What defined the action as "faith"? It was an action taken because God said to take it!
>
> When God spoke and a human acted on what He said, His power became visible on the earth. The invisible became visible through the faith-responses of humans.
>
> —Jennifer Kennedy Dean, *Live a Praying Life*

Examine the eternal record—the Scripture—for a consistent pattern of how the Word of God moved from invisible to visible through actions of faith. The writer of Hebrews states: "We do not want you to become lazy, but to imitate those who through faith and patience inherit what has been promised" (Hebrews 6:12). We are to examine the lives of those who exhibited faith so that we can imitate them. We can't look at every example the Scripture gives, so we will look at some representative examples.

Get out your Bible and open it to Exodus 7. The introduction to the drama about to unfold is in verses 1 through 6.

> *Then the LORD said to Moses, "See, I have made you like God to Pharaoh, and your brother Aaron will be your prophet. You are to say everything I command you, and your brother Aaron is to tell Pharaoh to let the Israelites go out of his country. But I will harden Pharaoh's heart, and though I multiply my miraculous signs and wonders in Egypt, he will not listen to you. Then I will lay my hand on Egypt and with mighty acts of judgment I will bring out my divisions, my people the Israelites. And the Egyptians will know that I am the LORD when I stretch out my hand against Egypt and bring the Israelites out of it."* **Moses and Aaron did just as the LORD commanded them.**
>
> —Exodus 7:1–6

Before the narrative opens, describing each of the encounters between Pharaoh and Moses and Aaron, do you see that God is announcing what He has available? He is describing the power and provision that He has at the ready. He assures them upfront that even when things look discouraging, all is going according to His plan. No matter what Moses and Aaron see, they can be sure that God is in charge. He impregnates them with promise. He paints a picture in their minds of what they can ultimately expect.

Notice, too, that an essential element of His plan is what Moses and Aaron will do in response to His voice. Now, read the familiar story, but read it with new eyes. Find it in Exodus 7:6–11, then skip to Exodus

12:29–36. Maybe you will want to go to your Bible computer program, if you have one, and copy and paste this section in a word processing program so you can print it out and scribble all over it. Look for the following points.

1. At what point in each encounter did Moses and Aaron know what God wanted them to do? Did God tell them obedience by obedience, in the moment? Or did He lay out His whole plan in detail from the beginning?

2. Underline every time you see the phrase, "just as the Lord had commanded." How did Moses and Aaron decide what to do or say at each encounter with Pharaoh?

3. In each encounter, notice that Moses and Aaron were to say something and to do something. If you have printed out the passage and can mark it up, draw an arrow to each phrase and write "SAY" or "DO." Just for fun, write it in a new color.

4. In each encounter, did God's power come into the environment of earth before or after Moses and Aaron obeyed, both in word and deed? Mark the phrases that tell you there was cause and effect between Moses' and Aaron's obedience and the visible demonstration of God's power.

5. As you look at each encounter, consider this: if Moses and Aaron did not have a picture to look at on the inside of them, what would the circumstances on the outside have looked like? Based on the observable facts—the empirical evidence—how might they have interpreted the outcome of each encounter? Beside the description of each encounter, write something that you will understand, like "good" or "bad." Or draw a smiling face or a frowning face. (Isn't this fun? Did you like to color when you were little? Does this bring it all back?)

6. Identify the instances where there seemed to be progress, but then things reversed and Moses and Aaron must have been disappointed. Put some identifying mark or word by those incidents.

7. Identify all the times that Moses' enemy tried to placate him by suggesting a compromise—a partial obedience.

8. In the end, did God bring about exactly the vision He had put inside Moses and Aaron?

Imitate the Faithful: Moses and Aaron

What can we learn about how faith functions from this pivotal event in Israel's history?

Faith begins with the voice of God. He impregnates you with promise, giving you certainty about what He wants to do, but not how He will do it. Your job is to obey moment by moment. Say what He tells you to say and do what He tells you to do. God has designed faith to work this way. This moment by moment following will require you to form a desperate dependence on God, clinging to Him and looking to Him every second.

Often we are unsettled by not knowing what the next step will be. We may be anxious when we can only see the step in front of us. But that is by deliberate design. Recently I was driving on an unfamiliar and poorly lit road at night in a dense fog. I could only see the road a few feet in front of me. My only hope was to keep moving in the light I had, knowing that as I moved the light would reveal the next little patch of road. The only way to know what the next step would be was to take the step in front of me. Every now and then, another car would be in front of me. Then I could see the patch my lights illuminated and a little bit of the patch the next car's lights illuminated. When someone was in front of me, I could "imitate" him and see a little more. But even then, the only option was to keep moving. As I drove through the fog, the situation forced me to be alert and focused, when usually my mind would be wandering to a thousand other things.

This is exactly how God has engineered faith to work.

Faith forces you to move forward, and you can only know that it is forward because God says it is. When I was driving in the fog, because my perspective was narrowed to what I could see in front of me, I often felt as if I were going backward. As you move in faith, forward might sometimes *feel* backward. Moses and Aaron had several instances during their obedience when it appeared that things took a turn for the worse. But they knew they were going *toward* the vision.

Faith is expressed in obedience. Each time that Moses and Aaron obeyed God's voice, their act of faith released the invisible Word of God to become visible on the earth. For example: "The Lord said to Moses and Aaron, 'When Pharaoh says to you, "Perform a miracle," then say to Aaron, "Take your staff and throw it down before Pharaoh," and it will become a snake.' *So Moses and Aaron went to Pharaoh and did just as the Lord commanded.* Aaron threw his staff down in front of Pharaoh and his officials, and it became a snake" (Exodus 7:8–10). After the obedience, the manifestation of the promise occurs. This is always the pattern.

Faith has an enemy. Your enemy is continually working against your faith, but he can only defeat you if he can discourage you. He is not in charge. Pharaoh thought he was in charge, but it is clear from the beginning that he was not.

It's not that you are growing in faith, as we often say, but that faith is growing in you. Your enemy is part of God's plan for growing faith in you. Everything your enemy tries can backfire on him and can deepen and strengthen your faith. That's what God uses him for.

As the confrontations between Moses and Aaron and the Pharaoh progressed, you can see the progressive weakening of their enemy as Moses and Aaron refused to give ground. In fact, his failure was put on display so that he was proven false and weak in the eyes of both his subjects and God's people.

The 10 plagues that God brought upon the enemy's territory were His plan from the outset. He fully intended that each of the 10 plagues would occur because each had a special focus in the enemy's camp. Let's look at them and see how faith stands firm until the enemy is fully exposed and deposed.

The first thing to notice is that the series of plagues begin and end with blood. The first plague is the turning of the Nile and all water into blood. The last is the blood of the lamb on the doorposts of the houses of the Israelites. Blood is the opening blow, from which the enemy never quite recovers his equilibrium, and blood is the final knock-out punch. The blood frames the battle, sets the parameters, draws the line. The enemy does not recognize that at the first appearance of the blood, his defeat is sure.

The first plague was the turning of the Nile into blood. The Nile was the life-blood of the nation of Egypt. Everything depended on the Nile. They worshiped the Nile and the Pharaoh was believed to be the personification of the Nile—the Nile made flesh, you might say. God's opening plague is a direct frontal assault on the very person of the enemy, establishing from the beginning who is God and who is not.

You need to know that God and your enemy are not in a fair fight. God is not picking on someone His own size. In the first round, the enemy is knocked senseless, even though he may not go down to stay until after a few more punches.

Each plague addresses directly one of Egypt's deities. The Egyptians had gods and goddesses for every aspect of their daily lives. Each plague showed God to be able to overpower every god of the Egyptians. The Egyptian gods, the people believed, empowered magicians. You notice that the magicians of Egypt were able to mimic the first plagues, but not completely reproduce them. For example, they could turn the water red, but they could not undo what they had done. They could call out frogs, but could not call them back. Quickly, the power of God outpaced the skills of the magicians.

As your vision is gestating, God will be taking on each stronghold that the enemy has in your life. His battle plan includes calling the enemy out from his hiding places, those cubbyholes where you have tucked away little idols. God wants to prove to you that He is able to add to your life what your idols promise but cannot deliver.

Don't let your enemy convince you that he has power over you. He does not. He only has the illusion of power. He postures and lies and deceives. He wants to entice you or bully you out of the realm of faith into the realm of fear and feelings. He wants to convince you to compromise—to obey, sort of. To half obey.

Your enemy needs to hear your voice. God commanded Moses and Aaron to speak the Word of the Lord to the enemy. I don't mean that you have to say words out loud, although it is not a bad idea when appropriate. Your thoughts are words and your enemy speaks in thoughts. And I don't necessarily mean that you have to address your words at the enemy. Declare in positive, declarative sentences what the Lord has promised you. It scares the enemy and it feeds your faith. Speak the Word that God has put in your mouth and send those living, active sound waves into the spiritual realm, where they cause reality to take on substance in the material realm.

The outcome is not in question. God declares the end from the beginning. When you are pregnant with promise, keep taking the picture that God has put in your mind out and looking at it.

He creates in you an understanding of circumstances in your life from His perspective. You can learn to look at the situation as it is on earth and see the situation as it will be when brought into contact with God's power.

Earth-perspective gives only a vague outline, and affords only a linear perspective. The earth point of view is like an artist's ébauche. An ébauche is the initial underpainting that establishes the broad lines of emphasis in a projected painting. It is unfinished. It is a rough outline only meant to establish the painting's basic components. The ébauche is never meant to be the finished work. If you were to mistake an artist's ébauche for his finished work, you would misjudge his talent. If you did not wait for the mature and finished work—if you walked away having seen only the ébauche—you would never truly see the painting. The finished work exists in the mind of the artist.

When you are using your spiritual vision, God will show you the finished work before it becomes available on the earth. It is already finished in His mind. Your Spirit-eyes will see it before your earth-eyes do. You will distinguish between an ébauche and a finished work of art. The circumstances on the earth are only the outline, alerting you to areas where God is going to complete the picture with His power.

Jehoshaphat's Ébauche

You will see this principle laid out in the story of Jehoshaphat found in 2 Chronicles 20:1–30. Open your Bible or print the passage out for study.

1. Identify the opening verses, 1–2, the situation as it appeared from the earth—the ébauche.

2. Underline the phrase that opens this account, "after this." After what? What preceded the enemy's attack?

3. How did Jehoshaphat interpret the ébauche? Did he embrace it as the finished picture?

4. How did he react to the facts on the ground? (verses 3–13)

5. As Jehoshaphat speaks truth and aligns his thinking with reality, what does he conclude? "We do not know what to do, but _____."

6. Why did Jehoshaphat fix his eyes upon God? Did he have confidence that God knew what he did not know?

7. Read verses 14–17. Was God's answer to Jehoshaphat's question

general? Or was it specific, detailed, and present tense?

8. God's answer to Jehoshaphat included directions about how Jehoshaphat was to proceed and what Jehoshaphat could confidently expect from God. God's power and provision would be released by Jehoshaphat's faith response. Identify what God commanded Jehoshaphat and what God promised Jehoshaphat.

9. Review the ébauche as presented in the first two verses. Now observe how the view changes as God paints His picture and impregnates Jehoshaphat with promise. (verses 15–17)

10. At what point did Jehoshaphat embrace the Lord's vision? After he had seen it in the material realm, or while it was still invisible? (verses 20–21)

11. Read how the promise looked when it became visible on the earth. Did it match the picture God had painted in Jehoshaphat's mind? (verses 22–27)

12. What was the response of Jehoshaphat and his people to seeing the picture they held in their minds take shape on the earth? What was the response of the enemy to the mighty work of God on behalf of His people? (verses 27–30)

Imitating the Faithful: Jehoshaphat

What can we learn about how faith functions from this event in the life of Jehoshaphat?

At times, God forces faith out of hiding by means of sudden situations. Jehoshaphat was not anticipating the attack that was looming on his horizon. Yet God had allowed the event in order to put His power on display and to cause faith to grow in His people.

In 2 Chronicles 20:1–2, Scripture first defines the earth-view of Judah's situation, the ébauche. "The Moabites and Ammonites with some of the Meunites came to make war on Jehoshaphat. Some men came and told Jehoshaphat, 'A vast army is coming against you from

Edom, from the other side of the Sea. It is already in Hazazon Tamar.'" Jehoshaphat, however, understood that this dire description of the facts did not constitute the whole of reality. "Alarmed, Jehoshaphat resolved to inquire of the LORD, and he proclaimed a fast for all Judah" (2 Chronicles 20:3). Jehoshaphat was "alarmed," but that alarm pushed him to seek God. He inquired of the Lord rather than take facts at face value. He inquired of the Lord because He knew God had something to impart to him that would give him direction.

When we seek Him, He reminds us of His promises, speaking them to us in the present tense. God began to fill Jehoshaphat's mind with His greatness. "O LORD, God of our fathers, are you not the God who is in heaven? You rule over all the kingdoms of the nations. Power and might are in your hand, and no one can withstand you" (2 Chronicles 20:6–12).

I know it might sound as if Jehoshaphat is reminding God, but really, God is reminding Jehoshaphat. God fills our minds with His Word so naturally that it feels as if we are saying it to Him, when, in reality, He is saying it to us. Sometimes, the listening comes in the speaking. You begin to express prayer and find that you spontaneously speak words that you had not consciously considered before, and you actually experience new insight as you hear your own prayer.

That very kind of thing happened to me just an hour ago. My three faithful intercessors—JoAnne, Wanda, and Mary—come to my house and pray for me and pray for the ministry the first Tuesday of every month. This morning, I was telling them about an obedience to which God had clearly called me that would involve a change of habit. I was saying that, in the abstract, it sounded fairly simple. However, when the first opportunity arose to obey, I found it to be hard. It made me recognize that something had more of a foothold in me than I knew. As we prayed, I was thanking God for His call to this obedience and for revealing to me that I had little idols tucked away in cubbyholes in my heart. I had never thought the word "cubbyholes" before nor had I thought the word "idols" in terms of my experience until I was praying and that was how I was picturing it. Wanda said, "Oh that is just what I was thinking because I'm reading a book and it says that the priests in the temple had little cubbyholes outside the temple where they hid their idols." (The book Wanda was reading is *The Key: How to Let Go and Let God* by Chuck and Nancy Missler.) It was such confirmation that God is actively directing our thoughts in harmony with His, and we loved it.

When they left, I came downstairs to my office and began working on this manuscript and immediately found myself writing about cubbyholes where we store our idols. This was exactly the thought needed at the very place that I was in the preparation of this manuscript. You just read that sentence a few pages back.

Faith is awakened by God voicing His Word. He was speaking His Word to Jehoshaphat, and Jehoshaphat was releasing it into the situation through prayer.

God's speaking brings the vision into focus. With every statement God's Spirit prompted in Jehoshaphat, his spiritual vision sharpened. He began to see the situation as it *would be*. God announced it to him through the mouth of the prophet Jahaziel: "Do not be afraid or discouraged because of this vast army. For the battle is not yours, but God's. Tomorrow march down against them....You will not have to fight this battle. Take up your positions; stand firm and see the deliverance the Lord will give you" (2 Chronicles 20:15b–17). Before this picture was finished on earth, it was finished in the spiritual realm. The situation on earth merely laid out the broad lines of emphasis where the power of God would be directly applied. The earth's circumstances just set the stage for the promise. Spiritual vision enables you to see that what God has promised He is bringing to pass. He "calls things that are not as though they were" (Romans 4:17b).

The enemy's attacks serve God's purposes. Because the assault of the enemy provided a platform for God's power, God had the opportunity to display His power and provision in a manner that would cause faith to grow in Jehoshaphat. If we never get to see God bring the finished painting out of the heavens and display it on the earth, then we won't learn to recognize an ébauche when we see one. We'll keep mistaking the ébauche for the painting.

Faith is obedience to the present voice of the Lord and sometimes the obedience is in not acting. God does not want your flesh in action. When Jehoshaphat obeyed the Lord's command not to attack, but instead to stand still and see the Lord work, all the power and provision of God flowed into the circumstances of earth.

Questions for Discussion

1. What does this mean? "The promise comes by faith."

2. Describe a situation in which faith has forced you to move forward.

3. Why does faith begin with the voice of God?

4. How does God often remind you of His faithfulness?

Chapter Ten

FAITH ON PARADE

By faith we understand that the universe was formed at God's command, so that what is seen was not made out of what was visible.

—Hebrews 11:3

Let me review what Hebrews 11:3 tells us, as we explored it in an earlier chapter. The material realm was made out of God's *rhema*. When God spoke, spiritual reality took on physical form. It became substance. This activity is the first, and therefore the primary, revelation of God—who He is and how He works. Every subsequent revelation builds on this foundation.

The Old Testament faithful are put on display as real-life lessons in how the faith principle operates. When God spoke, they acted in response to His voice, and God's power and provision flowed into the circumstances of earth and became visible.

Faith is more than how you deal with certain promises. It is a continual interaction with the spiritual realm. "My righteous one will *live* by faith" (Hebrews 10:38a). Faith is not a feeling you are required to stir up. Faith is not a static attendance to a set of theological beliefs. Faith is not something you get out and dust off when you want something from God. Faith is a way of living. Until it becomes a way of living, it will not be effective. *Faith is obeying the present-tense voice of the Father.* Faith is not believing something. Faith is *believing Someone.*

Think of faith as a spiritual organ through which you receive and use spiritual resources. In the earth-realm, for example, your eyes are the organ through which you receive light. Light is pressing in around you, but your eyes have to be open to receive it. Your lungs are the organ through which you receive oxygen. Oxygen is pressing in around you, but your lungs have to function in order to take it in. The Spirit-resources of heaven are available and pressing in around you, but you must live by faith in order to receive and use them.

You already have access to the eternal resources of God, the spiritual aspects of reality. Faith is how you take them into your life and use them. God's promises are not for someday. They're for today. Faith is not looking forward to a future so much as it is living fully supplied in the present.

> *For he **has rescued us** from the dominion of darkness and **brought us** into the kingdom of the Son he loves.*
> —Colossians 1:13

> *Praise be to the God and Father of our Lord Jesus Christ, who **has blessed us** in the heavenly realms with every spiritual blessing in Christ.*
> —Ephesians 1:3

> *And God **raised us up** with Christ and **seated us** with him in the heavenly realms in Christ Jesus.*
> —Ephesians 2:6

> *For you died, and your life **is now hidden** with Christ in God.*
> —Colossians 3:3

When God's Word speaks of the spiritual world, of the resources of the heavenly realm, the action is spoken of as already completed. Faith brings the available resources of God into our lives. The promise comes by faith.

As you boldly obey the present-tense voice of the Father, you access His power and provision. As you live the life to which you were born, you live in your inheritance. "Now if we are children, then we are heirs—heirs of God and co-heirs with Christ" (Romans 8:17a).

When faith is exercised on the earth, the power of God is released into the situation.

The writer of Hebrews says that the ancients were commended for their faith. It really means that they are witnesses to the reality of God's promise. Their experience attests to the certainty that faith in operation will access the promise. The promise comes by faith. If you want proof, look at the forefathers.

In each case, in the experiences of those to whom the writer of Hebrews directs our attention, faith was awakened by the voice of God, it was expressed through obedience to the present voice, and it resulted in the promise of God manifested in the circumstances of earth. God impregnated His people with promise, grew it in them as vision, and brought it through them as power and provision.

The eleventh chapter of Hebrews is about faith. Most of the chapter is about how faith looks in the lives of real people. Open your Bible to this chapter or print it out and start marking it up. As you go through it, mark the verbs—the action words—that faith produced. Let's take a more detailed look at some of the instances God highlights as prime examples of how faith looks and see if the pattern holds and the definition applies.

"By faith Abel offered God a better sacrifice than Cain did" (Hebrews 11:4a). How did Abel know what sacrifice would please God? He knew because God told him. If faith is what fueled Abel's action, then where did his faith come from? Faith comes only one way: "So faith comes from hearing, and hearing by the word (*rhema*) of Christ" (Romans 10:17 NASB).

Abel acted on what God told him. His obedience was called faith.

"By faith Enoch was taken from this life, so that he did not experience death" (Hebrews 11:5*a*). The author's argument is this: the Scripture testifies that Enoch walked with God so closely that his move from time into eternity required that his body simply change its form. One breath on earth, the next in eternity. Before he was taken, Enoch was "commended"—pointed out, highlighted—as "one who pleased God." Without faith, reasons the author, it is not possible to please God. God does not want your best efforts or your well-meaning actions. He wants your obedience to His voice. (See my book *Live a Praying Life*, Week 10, Day 5, page 175, for a fuller explanation of this verse.) Since one cannot please God without faith, and since Enoch pleased God, then Enoch's life and its translation into eternity evidenced his faith.

If you are bored by word study, skip this paragraph! A side note on Enoch: The Greek word (*methistemi*) translated "taken" and "taken away," or in the King James Version, "translated," is the same Greek word used in Colossians 1:13: "For he has rescued us from the dominion of darkness and brought us (*methistemi*) into the kingdom of the Son he loves." The Hebrew word this Greek word is interpreting is a word that has as one of its meanings "to remove boundaries." The word used in the King James, "translate," expresses the sense well. The word "translate" is from the Latin *trans* (across) and *latus* (to carry)—to carry across. When you translate a word from one language to another, you carry it across boundaries. That is what God did with Enoch. He removed the boundaries of earth from his body. That is what God has already done for your sprit. He has translated you into the kingdom and the life you live in your earth-bound body is not limited to what earth can offer. You are living a translated existence, a boundless life.

"By faith Noah…built an ark" (Hebrews 11:7). How did Noah decide to build an ark? Did he say to himself, "I'll bet God would be pleased if I just dropped everything and built an ark. You never know when an ark might come in handy." No—God told Noah to build an ark. The story of Noah found in Genesis says over and over, "And Noah did all that the LORD commanded him" (Genesis 7:5). God calls this faith. God put a picture in Noah's mind of the promise that faith would bring into the earth (Genesis 7:1–4) and Noah did all that the Lord commanded him. The picture that God painted for Noah, the promise with which He impregnated him, came to be on the earth on its due date. "In the six hundredth year of Noah's life, on the seventeenth day of the second month—on that day all the springs of the great deep burst forth, and the floodgates of the heavens were opened" (Genesis 7:11).

The author summarizes Abel, Enoch, and Noah. He is just getting warmed up. Then he moves to the patriarchs—the founding fathers. He puts more detail into these examples.

Faith Releases the Power of God

"*By faith* Abraham, when called to go…obeyed and went" (Hebrews 11:8). Who initiated Abraham's journey? God called Abraham, Abraham obeyed, and God called it faith.

"The LORD had said to Abram, 'Leave your country, your people and your father's household and go to the land I will show you'" (Genesis 12:1). The Hebrew would be more accurately translated, "go to a land I will *cause you to see*." The Lord paints a picture of the promise in Abraham's mind and then assured Abraham that God will cause him to see it. Abraham's response? "So Abram left, *as the LORD had told him*" (Genesis 12:4a). Fueled by faith.

"By faith he made his home in the promised land like a stranger in a foreign country; he lived in tents, as did Isaac and Jacob, who were heirs with him of the same promise. For he was looking forward to the city with foundations, whose architect and builder is God" (Hebrews 11:9–10). Even though the circumstances of Abraham's life gave no evidence that the land was his, he knew that it was. Everybody else thought the land belonged to the Canaanites, but Abraham knew it belonged to him. He was content to live as if he were a stranger in a foreign country because he had the certainty of God's word. He was looking forward—the word means "to accept or to receive"—to the dwelling place God would design and build for him. There is no contextual reason to interpret this as looking for heaven. Rather, it clearly means that Abraham lived in his present circumstances but was pregnant with the promise of God. Even though his current situation looked from the earth as if he were a visitor in the land, in Abraham's mind he had conceived the promise and that was his reality. He kept his thoughts focused on the reality of the promise rather than the illusion of the momentary situation. Matthew Henry said, "Faith demonstrates to the eye of the mind the reality of those things which cannot be discerned by the eye of the body."

"By faith even Sarah herself received ability to conceive, even beyond the proper time of life, since she considered Him faithful who had promised. Therefore there was born even of one man, and him as good as dead at that, as many descendants *as the stars of heaven in number, and innumerable as the sand which is by the seashore*" (Hebrews 11:11–12 NASB). (For this passage, I am switching the New American Standard because I am convinced

God's promises are not for someday. They're for today.

this is more accurate.) Sarah "received power"—the same word used for "received power" in Acts. She was impregnated with the promise to become pregnant with a son. She received the power. She took what was offered to her. She was given the miraculous power to conceive "*since*" (because) she counted on God to deliver what He had promised. "*Therefore*" (as a result), the promise to Abraham, and by extension to Sarah, took on substance and was manifested in the realm of earth. Fueled by faith, Sarah took possession of that which God offered to her and the picture God had painted in her mind showed up in the environment of earth.

The writer of Hebrews inserts a parenthetical thought here, in verses 13–16. He says that all these people were still in a faith position when they died, not having seen the fullness of the promises. Their promises all find their fullness in Christ. They only saw enough of the promise and experienced enough of its manifestation on earth to embrace its fullness from afar. When they died, they found the reality of what God was putting on the earth already fully formed in heaven. By means of their faith, God had been bringing what was in heaven into the environment of earth.

Then the writer picks up where he had left off—with Abraham again. "By faith Abraham, when God tested him, offered Isaac as a sacrifice" (Hebrews 11:17*a*). I want to set verses 17 through 19 aside until the next section, where we will look carefully at them.

Moving to the next spotlighted life, we read, "By faith Isaac blessed Jacob and Esau in regard to their future" (Hebrews 11:20). Isaac spoke his vision into the lives of his sons. He counted on the promise as his reality. In his blessing, Isaac was describing the picture God had painted in his mind as if it were certain and sure. He called what was not as though it were.

When Isaac blessed his sons, he was tricked by Jacob, the younger son, into pronouncing the blessing that Isaac intended for the older son, Esau. When the trickery was discovered, Esau begged his father to bless him also. But here is how certain Isaac was about the reality of that which he saw in his mind and pronounced in the form of blessing on Jacob. "Isaac answered Esau, 'I *have made him* lord over you and have made all his relatives his servants, and I *have sustained him* with grain and new wine. So what can I possibly do for you, my son?'" (Genesis 27:37). Isaac considered the promise his reality.

"By faith Jacob, when he was dying, blessed each of Joseph's sons, and worshiped as he leaned on the top of his staff" (Hebrews 11:21). Jacob, Joseph's father, blessed Joseph's two oldest sons, announcing out loud over their lives the reality that he could see with his mind. Fueled by faith, he called what was not as though it were.

"By faith Joseph, when his end was near, spoke about the exodus of the Israelites from Egypt and gave instructions about his bones"

(Hebrews 11:22). Fueled by faith, as he was dying, Joseph spoke of the future events that God had shown him on the inside. At that time, Joseph's reputation was at its peak and he would have been given a grand and elaborate burial in Egypt. At that time, the Israelites had not been enslaved and in fact were prospering and growing in Egypt. But Joseph could see with his heart that which could not be seen with the eyes. He demanded that his bones be brought to Canaan for burial when the time came and spoke the reality of the exodus of Israel long before it occurred on the earth. He believed what God's Word had shown him. He acted in accordance with that reality.

"By faith Moses' parents hid him for three months after he was born, because they saw he was no ordinary child, and they were not afraid of the king's edict" (Hebrews 11:23). When Moses was born, God spoke a promise into the minds of his parents that had more influence over them than the king's edict. The vision that God implanted in them was the reality in which they acted, not the circumstances that tried to demand their attention. Fueled by faith, they embraced the promise.

"By faith Moses, when he had grown up, refused to be known as the son of Pharaoh's daughter. He chose to be mistreated along with the people of God rather than to enjoy the pleasures of sin for a short time. He regarded disgrace for the sake of Christ as of greater value than the treasures of Egypt, because he was looking ahead to his reward. By faith he left Egypt, not fearing the king's anger; he persevered because he saw him who is invisible. By faith he kept the Passover and the sprinkling of blood, so that the destroyer of the firstborn would not touch the firstborn of Israel" (Hebrews 11:24–28). By faith, Moses responded to the call of God on his life and made decisions based on what he saw with spiritual vision rather than what he saw with his physical eyes. He continued seeing "him who is invisible." That was the reality and the basis for all his actions. He lived according to the vision that God had placed in him. Fueled by faith.

"By faith the people passed through the Red Sea as on dry land" (Hebrews 11:29a). Moses led the children of Israel out of Egypt. Following God's voice, they found themselves in an impossible situation. As they were camped by the Red Sea, they looked up to see Pharaoh's army advancing toward them. Looking at the situation in the material realm, they saw no escape. Moses, however, wasn't looking at the material realm. "He persevered because he saw him who is invisible" (Hebrews 11:27b). Moses had spiritual vision.

Read Exodus 14:1–12. You will see that God was leading the Israelites into this seemingly impossible situation for a definite purpose: "I will gain glory for myself through Pharaoh and all his army and the Egyptians will know that I am the LORD" (Exodus 14:4). God already had a plan. He knew what He wanted to do to save Israel. He had already planned to open the Red Sea and let Israel cross over on dry land. However, He didn't just do it. He said to Moses, "'Raise your staff and stretch out your hand over the sea to divide the water so the Israelites can go through the sea on dry ground.'…Then Moses stretched out his hand over the sea, and all that night the LORD drove the sea back…and turned it into dry land" (Exodus 14:15b–22).

What drove the sea back and turned it into dry land? It was not Moses' staff. Moses' staff had no power. God drove the sea back when Moses obeyed the present-tense voice of the Father. When he exercised faith, the power and provision of God showed up on the earth. Moses' faith-based obedience brought the fulfillment of the promise. The promise came by faith.

A similar incident occurred during Joshua's term of leadership. The story is found in Joshua 3. The Israelites needed to cross over the Jordan River. God said to Joshua: "'Tell the priests who carry the ark of the covenant: 'When you reach the edge of the Jordan's waters, go and stand in the river'" (Joshua 3:8). What happened when they obeyed the present-tense voice of God? "As soon as the priests who carried the ark reached the Jordan and their feet touched the water's edge, the water from upstream stopped flowing. It piled up in a heap a great distance away" (Joshua 3:15–16). Faith released the power and provision of God. The promise came by faith.

"By faith the walls of Jericho fell, after the people had marched around them for seven days" (Hebrews 11:30). Consider the example of Joshua found in Joshua 6. As the Israelites were taking possession of the land God had given them, they needed to take the city of Jericho. Jericho was protected by a high and impenetrable wall. "Now Jericho was tightly shut up because of the Israelites. No one went out and no one came in" (Joshua 6:1). What would collapse the walls of Jericho? Would military might? Physical strength? Clever strategy? Courage?

None of these things would do the job. It would take a mightier force than existed in the material realm. "By faith the walls of Jericho fell" (Hebrews 11:30*a*). Nothing but faith would collapse the fortress around Jericho.

How did this wall-tumbling faith operate? "Then the LORD said to Joshua, 'See, I have delivered Jericho into your hands'" (Joshua 6:2*a*). In the material realm, nothing had changed. Jericho's wall was just as strong as it had always been. The odds were against Israel—or so it appeared. Notice that God did not say "I *will deliver* Jericho," but "I *have delivered* Jericho into your hands." God called what was not as though it were. Then He told Joshua exactly how to bring the victory out of heaven and establish it on the earth. You can read God's directives in verses 3 through 5. Joshua and the people did exactly as God had commanded. They were obedient to the present-tense voice of God. God called it faith, and it brought the promise. "By faith the walls of Jericho fell, after the people marched around them for seven days" (Hebrews 11:30). Wall-tumbling faith is lived out in dynamic, active, bold obedience to God's voice.

"By faith the prostitute Rahab, because she welcomed the spies, was not killed with those who were disobedient" (Hebrews 11:31). When Joshua was preparing the Israelites to take the city of Jericho, he sent two spies in to scout out the terrain. They were taken in by a woman named Rahab. Most English translations call her a prostitute, but the same word—both in Hebrew and the Greek word used here—is more often translated "innkeeper." If she was a prostitute, she was also an innkeeper, and she took in the two spies. The king of Jericho got wind of the spies' presence in Rahab's house and he sent a command to her to produce them. She lied and said that she had turned them away. Then she crept up to the roof where she had hidden them and told them something that their eyes could not see.

> Before the spies lay down for the night, she went up on the roof and said to them, "I know that the LORD has given this land to you and that a great fear of you has fallen on us, so that all who live in this country are melting in fear because of you. We have heard how the LORD dried up the water of the Red Sea for you when you came out of Egypt, and what you did to Sihon and Og, the two kings of the Amorites east of the Jordan, whom you completely destroyed. When we heard of it, our hearts melted and everyone's courage failed because of you, for the LORD your God is God in heaven above and on the earth below."
>
> —Joshua 2:8–11

God had shown the inhabitants of the land that He had given the land to the Israelites. Rahab could see the truth and she obeyed the truth. She lived in the reality of the truth. Everyone else was disobedient. Rahab's obedience to the reality that God had revealed to her resulted in her salvation and the salvation of her family. Fueled by faith, she lined herself up with God's promise and the promise came by faith.

The definition remains consistent. God calls things that are not as though they were. He talks about the eternal truth, not the appearance of the moment. God does not direct your attention to the need but to the supply. Before a need enters your experience, God has fully prepared the supply. Your faith will get the finished work of God out of heaven and onto earth.

What are the circumstances in your life that look overwhelming and impossible? Now place them against the backdrop of the amazing power and astonishing love of God. Do they look different now? Do you see them as they are? Every circumstance, every need, every desire is God's entry point into your life. Every difficulty is simply highlighting the exact place where God will apply His power. Every challenge or obstacle is God's opportunity to substantiate His promises. Problems are nothing more than labor pains as God brings about the birth of His vision.

The truth is this: every mountain becomes a road. Every desert abounds with streams and pools of water. Lush gardens grow in the wastelands. Treasures are hidden in the darkness.

In each case, God initiated the call and the faith-hero responded in obedience to God's present-tense voice. In every case, the obedience provided God the opportunity to show His power on earth.

Questions for Discussion

1. In Hebrews 11, God spotlights certain lives and holds them out as examples of faith. What is the common thread in each?

2. God is spotlighting your life right now, holding you out as proof to those around you. Describe situations in your life right now that are forcing faith into the open.

Chapter Eleven

THE SCIENCE OF FAITH

Now faith is being sure of what we hope for and certain of what we do not see.
—Hebrews 11:1

E verything we looked at in the previous chapter was introduced by this sentence. This is the thesis statement—the concept that is to be proven and documented in the sentences that follow. Everything the author states in Hebrews 11 is a foundation for this definition of faith.

The words in this pithy statement are solid, massive, substantial words. The words have to do with certainty, not guessing. They depict knowing, not wishful thinking. Do you recall Paul's words from Ephesians 1:18? "I pray also that the eyes of your heart may be enlightened in order that you may *know*." That is, that you may fully comprehend and understand and grasp and lay hold of.

Faith is not subjective. It is not believing something for which no evidence exists. It is, in fact, the very opposite. It is recognizing the evidence when you see it.

Briefly, let me recap some thoughts. God's promise comes (is transported by) faith. That which exists in the spiritual realm in a finished state is moved into the material realm by faith. Faith is the technique by which we access and make use of all the provision of God.

Faith is obedience to the present-tense voice of God.

The words used in this straightforward definition of faith are words of science. The King James Version translates it, "Now faith is the substance of things hoped for, the evidence of things not seen." That is the wording I want to work from as we allow the Holy Spirit to unlock the riches stored in the secret places.

Faith Is the Substance

Hebrews 11:1 uses physics terms to define faith. The goal of physics is to test and prove what is real. In physics, a discovery is not creating something new, but it is proving the reality of what already exists. "Faith is the substance of things hoped for" (Hebrews 11:1*a* KJV).

The word "substance" (*hupostasis*) means "the substantial nature of a thing; the real nature or the essence of a thing that supports its outward forms; material from which something is made; the chemical composition of an element." It means what something is made up of. What is the reality behind the manifestation?

"Things hoped for" (*elpizo*) means "to confidently expect; to anticipate." The English word "hope" does not communicate this well. "Expect" might be a better word. The kind of hope about which the Bible speaks is a certainty, not a wish.

For example, my husband just now called to tell me that he is a few minutes from home. He is not home right now, but I am certain that he will be home at some yet undetermined moment. He is headed toward home and every minute that elapses, he is closer to home. So I am going to go upstairs and set the table for dinner and get the meal out of the oven and pour water into the glasses. He said he was almost home, so I expect him home. That is the kind of hope the Scripture portrays.

What is it that we can hope for, or confidently expect? That which God has promised. How has He brought that promise to life? By implanting it as vision. So the phrase "things hoped for" can be translated "the vision."

We have already assigned a definition to the word "faith" and have looked at Scripture to see that the definition will hold up. Faith is obedience to the present voice of God.

The writer of Hebrews uses language in this statement that might be used to state a scientific formula. The word translated "substance" means "that which stands under; the essence or make-up of." We would use this word to say, for example, "H_2O is the substance of water." What makes up water? H + H+ O. We would write it out as a scientific equation something like this:

H_2O *is the substance of* water.

H_2O = water

Every time H+H+O come together—every single time without fail—water is the result. Why? Because *H_2O is the substance of water.*

Follow the same logic as we look at the statement, "Faith is the substance of things hoped for." It is the same kind of language. Let's give faith a symbol, so we can see the equation in its scientific form. Let's call "faith" OPV (obedience to the present voice). Let's call "things hoped for" the vision. Our formula would look like this:

Faith (OPV) *is the substance of* **things hoped for (the vision).**

(OPV) = (the vision)

Every time we act on the present voice of God (faith), the promises of God (vision) are revealed on the earth.

If a scientific equation is accurate, it is true every single time without fail. A scientific formula is a statement of truth or a definition of reality.

The promises of God come from the spiritual end of the continuum of reality, heaven, to the material end of the continuum, earth, by the exercise of faith. When you live by faith—a life marked by obedience—then the vision inside you will begin to take on substance in the material realm.

The call that God has placed in your life, the vision that He has implanted in your imagination, is also a promise. He will bring it about. He will provide for every need in relation to the call. He will provide your passion, your insight, your clear understanding. He will open every door. He will give the finances. He will provide what you need when you need it as you walk out the call, always listening to His now-speaking voice. Every time you act in faith, you give substance to God's promises. "And God is able to make all grace abound to you, so that in all things at all times having all that you need, you will abound in every good work" (2 Corinthians 9:8).

The Evidence

Faith is…the evidence of things not seen.

—Hebrews 11:1 KJV

Once again, let's define our terms. The word translated "evidence" is *elegchos* and it means "prove by demonstration; convince by proving; prove, investigate, persuade."

The word "things" is the word *praga,* and it means strictly "things done; an accomplished fact." It does *not* mean "items," or, as we in the United States might say, "stuff." You may recognize it as the root of our English word "pragmatic," which means "having to do with matters of fact or actual occurrence." The "things not seen" then are those things that God has already accomplished and are in a ready form but are not revealed in the environment of earth. For every situation or challenge that confronts you, God has a ready, finished answer available. (To explore this concept in more detail, see *He Leads Me Beside Still Waters* by Jennifer Kennedy Dean.) He is never scrambling to scrape something together. His activity is always moving finished work out of the spiritual realm and into the earth's experience.

The word "seen" is *blepo* and means to discern with the bodily eye. Things not seen are not visible to the physical senses. "Things not seen" could be translated as "the vision"—the promise God has put into you and caused you to see with your mind.

With those definitions in place, examine our contention that faith is the evidence of things not seen. Faith proves the existence of an invisible reality. Again, the writer uses a word that would be used in discussing science.

For every situation or challenge that confronts you, God has a ready, finished answer available.

Scientists have a way of observing phenomena with a curious eye. Everything they can see hints to them of something that they can't see. Everything they can see is *being caused* by something they can't see. The basic law of physics is "Effect proceeds from cause." In other words, if something happens, something caused it to happen. The effective power is not in the event you can see, but in the causing event that you can't see. The statement that faith is "evidence of things not seen" is the statement of a logical, rational, scientific thought.

The language of the sentence is the same kind of language a scientist would use to say, "The experiment proves the unseen cause." A scientist will take note of a phenomenon—an event that you can observe. Then he will speculate, based on all he knows to be true, as to what might be causing that phenomenon. He develops a hypothesis. Now what does he have to do? He has to put his hypothesis to the test. If his hypothesis proves consistently to be true, then his idea has moved from being hypothesis to being fact. The experiment *is the evidence of* the reality.

The experiment provides convincing evidence that the hypothesis is true. The experiment proves the reality.

The experiment *is the evidence of* the hypothesis. The hypothesis (things that are yet not seen, but are nonetheless true) is proven to be fact and truth by means of the experiment.

The experiment tests and *proves* the hypothesis. Every time the experiment is reproduced correctly, it produces the same results, proving that the hypothesis is true.

Every time the experiment is performed—every single time without fail—the hypothesis is substantiated. Why? Because *the experiment is the evidence of the hypothesis.*

Now, apply the same logic and thought processes to the statement, "Faith is the evidence of things not seen."

Faith proves the reality of those things not seen, heard, or understood by the human senses. "'No eye has seen, no ear has heard, no mind has conceived what God has prepared for those who love him'—but God has revealed it to us by his Spirit" (1 Corinthians 2:9–10).

Faith provides convincing evidence that the things not seen truly exist.

Every time faith (OPV) operates, it produces the same results—the vision takes on substance and becomes visible in the material realm—proving that the promises are real.

Every time faith (OPV) is exercised on the earth—every single time without fail—it gives God the opportunity to prove His promises. Why? Because *faith is the evidence of the vision.*

The promises are proven to be fact by the exercise of faith. Faith *proves* the things not seen.

Faith *is the evidence of* things not seen.

Since the promise comes by faith, until faith is expressed, the promise will be blocked. Conversely, every time faith is expressed, the promise will become experience. Do you long for the promises of God to be part of your daily experience? Prove them. Act on the present-tense voice of the Father. Live by His Word. Make the confession of Mary your confession: "I am the Lord's servant....May it be to me as you have said" (Luke 1:38). Give God every opportunity to prove the vision is a reality.

Questions for Discussion

1. How can you put faith to the test and prove its reality?

2. How does the vision that God has given you come from the invisible realm to the visible realm?

Chapter Twelve

FAITH THAT REASONS

"Come now, let us reason together," says the LORD.

—Isaiah 1:18

Often we are told that faith and reason are mutually exclusive. The word "faith," in western vernacular, has come to mean believing something in the absence of proof or evidence. It has the sense of an arbitrary, unfounded, impulsive decision, like grasping at straws. Faith is considered by many to be a position of weakness or passivity, an escape from reality.

Are you already seeing that this does not line up with Scripture's definition of faith? Faith is active, bold, aggressive, fearless, well-founded, and utterly reasonable. Faith is reason in its highest form. Faith is logic at its purest.

As God has revealed Himself in creation, one thing He has made visible is the astonishing, breath-taking orderliness and cohesiveness of His mind. The perfection of the universe—one part fitting perfectly into another, even the smallest piece essential to its working, nothing out of place—is beyond imagining. If His creation reveals Him, then it reveals reasoning as a divine attribute. Jesus is "Logic (*logos*) Made Flesh."

What is logic? It is a thought process in which fact is laid upon fact, building to a conclusion. It is stacking concept upon concept until a fully formed thought emerges. Isn't that exactly the process by which

God progressively revealed Himself to His people? He began in the Old Covenant introducing them to one concept, then added the next and fitted the two together, then the next, and the next, and the next. Then, at the fullness of time, timed perfectly in the stream of revelation, all the thoughts of God were revealed in the flesh as Jesus—in whom all the fullness of the Deity lived in bodily form (Colossians 2:9)—broke into time and space as the Logos of God.

The reason that human logic and faith so often are at odds is because when your logic—your stacked-up, lined-up thoughts—has a wrong starting point, or has an untruth somewhere along the line, it will also have a wrong ending point. That is why I say that faith is logic in its highest form and reasoning at its purest. Truth upon truth upon truth will reach, as its conclusion, Truth.

The Textbook Case

This incident in Abraham's life is the textbook definition of faith.

> *By faith Abraham, when God tested him, offered Isaac as a sacrifice. He who had received the promises was about to sacrifice his one and only son, even though God had said to him, "It is through Isaac that your offspring will be reckoned." Abraham **reasoned** that God could raise the dead, and figuratively speaking, he did receive Isaac back from death.*
>
> —Hebrews 11:17–19

The writer of Hebrews is writing commentary on the Scripture, explaining Old Testament events in the light of New Testament reality. The writer, again, uses a word associated with science to define the thought process of Abraham that led him to faith.

From *Discover* magazine (July 2002), "Believing in Science," look at the following statements: "Science requires an interesting kind of faith.... No one has seen an electron or a quark or a proton or a neutrino. We assume subatomic particles based on heaps of experimental evidence, but we don't have instruments sensitive enough to allow us to pick up one of them and stare at it."

What a scientist does is line up the proven facts all the way out to the end and then make the next logical assumption. If A is true, and B is true, then C must be true. He *reasons*. Then, he puts his assumption to the test. He tries it out to see if it holds up. What he reasons to be true based on what he knows to be true becomes *fact* to him. His world—the environment in which he lives and moves and has his being—is based on his *facts*, as he knows them. These facts are his truth, his reality.

Abraham used a scientific technique in reaching a solid conclusion about the reliability of God's promise, which enabled him to act on God's present voice. He reasoned. He lined up every truth he knew, stacked them one on top of the other, and then reached the only possible conclusion. He inventoried everything he knew to be true—he cataloged it—and it led him to one possibility. He took inventory of everything that had already been proven true. He put the present call of God into his inventory.

Abraham lined up the facts he knew and from them deduced what he did not know. He thought something along these lines: "God is good. God is faithful to His covenant. God promised me a son through whom a nation would be born. Isaac is the very son God promised me. God has named Isaac as the one through whom the promise would come to its fulfillment. God has commanded me to take Isaac, my only son, and offer him as a sacrifice on the altar. That will require his life. When I obey God, Isaac will be dead." Now Abraham makes the next logical assumption: "Abraham reasoned that God could raise the dead."

Abraham was confronted with an unknown. The present voice of God was speaking to him: "'Take your son, your only son, Isaac, whom you love, and go to the region of Moriah. Sacrifice him there as a burnt offering on one of the mountains I will tell you about" (Genesis 22:2).

To get to faith—obeying the present voice—Abraham reasoned. From what he had already seen, he reached a conclusion about what he could not see. He reasoned that God could raise the dead. That became fact and reality to him when he put it to the test. Faith did not come into play until "By faith Abraham...*offered* Isaac" (Hebrews 11:17).

Abraham was fully convinced in his own mind. By the processes of reasoning that God led Abraham through, he came out with a picture in his mind of the promise of God. That vision had Isaac in it. We can see how sure Abraham was that the vision was the reality by this account:

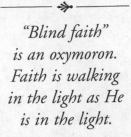

"Blind faith" is an oxymoron. Faith is walking in the light as He is in the light.

"On the third day Abraham looked up and saw the place in the distance. He said to his servants, 'Stay here with the donkey while I and the boy go over there. We will worship and then *we will come back to you*'" (Genesis 22:4–5).

The writer of Hebrews said that indeed Abraham did receive Isaac back, as if from the dead. Indeed Abraham did see God perform a type of resurrection. "Figuratively speaking, he did receive Isaac back from death" (Hebrews 11:19*b*).

When Abraham acted on the voice of God (OPV), that which he had deduced as true and acted on as true was proved to be true. His faith (OPV) was the element that caused the promise of God to take on substance in the material realm. God's promise was moved from the spiritual realm into the material realm through Abraham's faith. **The promise came by faith.**

God invites you to come to Him so you can reason together. "'Come now, let us reason together,' says the LORD" (Isaiah 1:18). The word translated "reason" is a word often used to describe a court case. God says, "Come to Me and let's lay out our arguments side by side. You make your case, and I'll make My case. I'll hear you fully and you'll hear Me fully. When our reasoning is put out where we can see it and compare it, Mine will convince you. You'll see what I see. Come, let us reason together." God wants us to understand as much as our minds can possibly understand. He wants to help you see where your reasoning has missed the mark and to put you back into truth.

God wants to bring you understanding. "Blind faith" is an oxymoron. Faith is walking in the light as He is in the light. Faith is living with the eyes of your heart enlightened so you will *know*. He has given us His Spirit so that we can *know* what is freely available to us in the spiritual realm.

In faith, you are walking blind in the sense that you don't see the whole road ahead of you. You see step by step.

As you obey Him, He will reveal wisdom as you need it. The wise heart will know what it needs to know when it needs to know it. God will make the right thing known at the right time.

"I will lead the blind by ways they have not known, along unfamiliar paths I will guide them; I will turn the darkness into light before them and make the rough places smooth. These things I will do; I will not forsake them" (Isaiah 42:16).

God promises that He will lead you as if He were leading a blind person along unfamiliar paths. A blind person can manage well along familiar paths, but he has no way to safely navigate unfamiliar paths. One who is leading a blind person by ways he has not known will be guiding and directing each step, each movement. The guide will be moving obstacles and smoothing the way. The guide will not leave the blind person on his own even momentarily. He will be protecting the blind person from dangers he cannot see. The blind person will rely on the sight of his guide. He will put all his trust in his guide. As long as the blind person is in the guide's care, his disability does not limit him. He is tapping into the guide's ability and that's all he needs.

As you obey God's commands, all you have to do is rely fully on Him. Your inability does not matter. God doesn't shrink the size of His power to fit within your abilities; He expands your abilities to accommodate the size of His power. His power is most visible in your weakness. As Paul says, rejoice in your weaknesses—embrace them, celebrate them. They are the perfect background against which God can display His power. Your weaknesses will compliment His power perfectly.

—Jennifer Kennedy Dean, *Riches Stored in Secret Places*

However, your response of faith is not blind. It is fully enlightened. You choose to be led a step at a time by the One whom your heart sees clearly.

Questions for Discussion

1. What does it mean that Abraham "reasoned that God could raise the dead"?

2. To what circumstances in your life right now do you need to apply reasoning faith?

Chapter Thirteen

THE FAITH FACTOR

The knowledge of the secrets of the kingdom of heaven has been given to you.
—Matthew 13:11

How can you know that what you see in your mind is from God and not from your own imagination? Is that what you are wondering right now? That is a question you should always ask because we need to be skeptical of our own flesh. But don't let yourself be paralyzed by it. Deal with it and then move on in faith.

Let me give you my own check-points for the source of vision in my life. First, let the Spirit perform this echocardiogram on your heart.

Is your heart's desire to do the will of God? Jesus said, "If anyone chooses to do God's will, he will find out whether my teaching comes from God or whether I speak on my own" (John 7:17). The person who wants to know God's desires will know God's desires.

"I am the good shepherd; I know my sheep and my sheep know me—just as the Father knows me and I know the Father—and I lay down my life for the sheep" (John 10:14–15). Jesus promised that you do know Him the same way He knows the Father. You can follow Him the same way He followed the Father. Jesus *promised*. **Do you believe that?**

"When he, the Spirit of truth, comes, he will guide you into all truth. He will not speak on his own; he will speak only what he hears, and he will tell you what is yet to come. He will bring glory to me by taking from what is mine and making it known to you" (John 16:13–14). **Do you trust that the Sprit of God who indwells you will guide you into all truth and tell you even things that are yet to come?** By that, I don't mean that He will become your personal fortune-teller or satisfy your curiosity about the future. But He will reveal to you things yet to come insofar as that revelation is necessary for instilling faith.

Settle these issues, then we can explore further ways that you can feel assured that your vision is from God and is His promise to you.

It is a given that what the Lord has personally promised to you will not contradict His revealed Word. It will be perfectly in line with the Scripture. With that as our launch pad, consider some other factors.

Built-In Vision

God's call and promise are the same. He who calls you also enables and empowers you. His call on your life is encoded in your DNA. You are put together in such a way that your whole being—your physical appearance, your emotional style, your personality type, your talents, your way of processing information, your sense of humor, your passions—all of you is the packaging for your vision. You were born to flesh out this vision. God is a strategic thinker, and He has carefully put you together and given you everything you need and timed your appearance on earth so that it all coincides with His vision for you.

Moses is a prime example. Many generations before Moses' birth, God told Abraham about Moses. "Then the LORD said to him, 'Know for certain that your descendants will be strangers in a country not their own, and they will be enslaved and mistreated four hundred years. But I will punish the nation they serve as slaves, and afterward they will come out with great possessions'" (Genesis 15:13–14). God did not mention Moses' name, but He revealed to Abraham what Moses would be called to do. He revealed that He had a timetable in place. At just the right moment in earth-time, a baby boy would be born to a particular Hebrew family. Stephen, in the Book of Acts, said this: "As the time drew near for God to fulfill his promise to Abraham....*At that time* Moses was born, and he was no ordinary child" (Acts 7:17, 20). Just at the time that all seemed lost, just at the time when events had reached critical mass for the Hebrew slaves in Egypt and God was ready to implement the next part of His plan, at that time, Moses was born.

Because God had a specific role for Moses to play, He strategically arranged all the details of his life. He was born to the people of God, but educated and trained in the ways of the Egyptians, the world's most powerful and advanced nation. "Moses was educated in all the wisdom of the Egyptians and was powerful in speech and action" (Acts 7:22). God made sure that Moses' life brought him into

> *God's call and promise are the same. He who calls you also enables and empowers you.*

contact with the training and the experiences and the relationships that would form him and fit him for the vision. Let me summarize some extra-biblical sources, historians Josephus, Philo, and Irenaeus. They are considered reliable historians, but this is not Scripture. So, though I don't give it the weight of Scripture, it is interesting and is supported by Scripture.

Moses was an extraordinarily beautiful child and handsome man. Josephus goes to great lengths to describe what a beautiful child he was, so beautiful that people stopped to stare at him. According to all of the writers, this was what caused the pharaoh's daughter to be so taken with him when she found him in the Nile and she wanted him as her own son. She had no children.

The method of Moses' appearance to the pharaoh's daughter seems to me to be significant in light of how the Egyptians believed that their great god Re appeared. "Re was the self-engendered Eternal Spirit who first appeared on the waters of the Nun (Nile) as a beautiful child floating on a great blue lotus" (Barbara Watterson, *Gods of Ancient Egypt*). This must also have been in her mind as she drew him out of the water. Since all pharaohs were believed to be gods, and the offspring of gods, perhaps the unusual way that she came upon him was even part of the way that the Divine Unseen Hand was directing events to their appointed outcome.

When Moses was grown, he was very tall and unusually strong. I think the Scripture bears that out when it tells us that he, alone, killed one of the Egyptian taskmasters. These taskmasters were chosen for their physical strength and for their brutality. Daily, they beat the Israelites. For Moses to be able to kill him would have required extraordinary strength.

Moses, according to the historians, was also extraordinarily intelligent and learned at such a pace that he surpassed his teachers. Both of these facts are attested to by Stephen when he says, "Moses was educated in all the wisdom of the Egyptians and was powerful in speech and action" (Acts 7:22).

Philo describes Moses this way: "But Moses, having now reached the highest point of human good fortune, and being looked upon as the grandson of this mighty king, and being almost considered in the expectations of all men as the future inheritor of his grandfather's kingdom, and being always addressed as the young prince..." (Translated by C.D. Yonge, *The Works of Philo*). According to the historians, it was well known that Moses was of Hebrew descent. Many Egyptians mistrusted him, thinking that he may someday side with the Hebrews. This clarifies for me how the writer of Hebrews defined Moses' faith when he says, "By faith Moses, when he had grown up, refused to be known as the son of Pharaoh's daughter. He chose to be mistreated along with the people of God rather than to enjoy the pleasures of sin for a short time. He regarded disgrace for the sake of Christ as of greater value than the treasures of Egypt, because he was looking ahead to his reward" (Hebrews 11:24–26). That had always confused me because I understood that Moses had been forced out of Egypt, rather than choosing to leave Egypt. However, both Philo and Josephus describe how Moses always felt compassion toward his kinsmen and even influenced the pharaoh to hand down edicts lessening the harsh treatment of the slaves, edicts which were for the most part ignored and not enforced. Maybe this is what finally pushed Moses to personally step in and rescue a slave. I think it was at that moment, when Moses took drastic action with his own hands, that he made a choice between his kinsmen and the riches of Egypt.

Philo says that the king was angry, not at the murder of one man by another, "but for his grandson not to agree with him, and not to look upon his friends or his enemies as his own, but to hate persons whom the king loved, and to love persons whom the king looked upon as outcasts, and to pity those whom he regarded with unchangeable and implacable aversion" (Yonge, *Philo*, 463). All the historians agree that Moses was held in such high regard by the king that he could probably have confronted his accusers and won the king's favor, but he had made his choice to align himself with his kinsmen instead and so turned his back on the power and the privilege that could have been his.

Do you see how Moses always had the vision, and it gestated over time? Do you see how God so designed Moses and then so directed the details of his life and engineered his experiences so that when the vision was due on the earth, everything about Moses was ready? Even his greatest failure, when he took God's plan into his own hands and committed murder, was essential in the birth of the vision.

Don't you imagine that when Moses had to flee Egypt and even his own people misunderstood him, he thought the vision was lost? The biblical account leads me to believe that Moses had buried the vision. He spent the next 40 years of his life tending sheep, obscure and unknown, in the scorching Arabian desert. During those 40 years, God performed soul-surgery on Moses. He took the flesh out of the vision, educated Moses in all the wisdom of the kingdom, and replaced his Moses-power with God-power. Even his failure and his desert time were hastening the vision toward its due date.

When God appeared to Moses in the burning bush, it was the combination of Moses' training in the ways of the One True God coupled with his knowledge of Egyptian superstitions that this encounter was designed to draw upon. You know the encounter well. Moses, seeking assurance, asked God, "What is your name?"

Let me set that against the background of Egyptian understanding of the names of their gods. Re was the Egyptian god who ruled both men and gods. The secret to Re's power was that no one knew "the Great Name of Re, his secret name....Re had many names, but the Great Name was the one that gave him power over gods and men. It had remained hidden in his body since his birth so that no magician might gain power over him" (Watterson, *Egypt*, 42). The Egyptians had many stories about lesser gods who tried to trick Re into revealing his hidden name.

Do you see that, even at that beginning of the labor pains, the One True God was showing Moses that He would readily reveal to Moses His Great Name, Jehovah? That spoke faith into Moses. Then God, who had revealed His Great Name to Moses, gave Moses a promise and described a picture that Moses could see in his mind. "And God said, 'I will be with you. And this will be the sign to you that it is I who have sent you: When you have brought the people out of Egypt, you will worship God on this mountain'" (Exodus 3:12). Through all the labor pains, Moses had a picture he could look at and believe. Promise implanted as vision.

God has been directing your life toward the vision all along. Look back and consider what you see. How have your circumstances, good and bad, been arranged so that the vision can grow? How have your particular challenges and failures and heartaches prepared you to host the vision?

Suited for the Vision

Notice that Moses was always a rescuer. It was his natural inclination. You can see it when he killed the Egyptian taskmaster to rescue a Hebrew slave. Although it seems to have been an impulsive decision in the moment, it must have been the eruption of pent-up anger and frustration. He had tried other ways to rescue the Hebrews and finally his drive to rescue drove him to a reckless act.

When Moses escaped into the desert, one of his first acts was to rescue. "Now a priest of Midian had seven daughters, and they came to draw water and fill the troughs to water their father's flock. Some shepherds came along and drove them away, but Moses got up and came to their rescue and watered their flock" (Exodus 2:16–17).

When you think of your vision, you realize that there is a certain drive in you. Albert Einstein, whose theory of relativity changed the face of physics by proving light to be traveling at a constant speed, used to daydream as a little child what it would be like to travel on a beam of light.

I can remember as a child, after listening to sermons or Sunday School lessons, I would go home and think them all through again and consider a better way to express it. I could see myself teaching from a platform. Of course, in those long-ago days, that was not a very realistic vision for a little girl to have. I didn't really embrace it as vision then because it was unheard of. I just thought of it as daydreaming. Yet that drive to dissect ideas and recast them, and that thirst to learn and then to teach, was too much a part of me to get rid of. Over the years, God opened door after door, and what I could see back then as a little girl is exactly my reality now.

Observe how God has suited you in temperament, in interests, in talents for the vision. What did you used to daydream about as a child? How did you cast yourself in your dreams? What is the desire that won't go away?

Opportunity Knocks

Notice that God has arranged along the way for you to have the opportunities to develop the skills and learn the information that you need for your vision to develop. He has placed in your path the people and the situations that have nourished the vision and allowed it to grow. You have come across opportunities in the most supernatural ways.

God uses "the knight's move" often—taking unexpected turns to get to a destination. "In a game of chess, the knight's move is unique because it alone goes around corners. In this way it combines the continuity of a set sequence with the discontinuity of an unpredictable turn in the middle. This meaningful combination of continuity and discontinuity in an otherwise linear set of possibilities has led some to refer to the creative act of discovery in any field of research as 'a knight's move' in intelligence" (James E. Loder and W. Jim Neidhardt, *The Knight's Move*, [Colorado Springs: Helmers & Howard Publishing, 1992], 2).

Let me tell you one of many, many stories when God used the knight's move to get me where He wanted me when He wanted me there. Some years ago, through speaking at an event, I developed a friendship with Susan and Rob Cottrell in Phoenix, Arizona. They are friends and encouragers of my ministry. Now, set Susan and Rob in Phoenix aside for a minute. In North Carolina, a women's ministry team for a particular church is trying to determine who its speaker will be for its annual conference, and the team is well past the time when this is usually decided. In the midst of this, one of the women leaves for a vacation. Another on her team, doing an Internet search stumbles across my Web site and calls our office to request information. She gets excited about the message and calls to see if that date is open for me. It happens to be the only open weekend on my calendar. She can't wait until her friend gets back from vacation so she can tell her whom she suggests as a speaker and see if her friend will agree. Meanwhile, her friend is flying back from her vacation and happens to be seated on an airplane next to my friend Rob Cottrell from Phoenix. They converse and discover their mutual faith, so the woman decides to ask Rob if he knows of any women speakers. Rob says, "Have you ever heard of Jennifer Kennedy Dean?" and he graciously tells her about me. When the two women get together, each now has someone she wants to suggest for the retreat. And, as it turns out, they each want to suggest Jennifer Kennedy Dean.

Time and time again, God will pull opportunities out of nowhere (so it seems) and will drop them in your lap and you will know that the vision is His and He is managing it. It will confirm the promise to you.

Checklist

☐ *Is your primary desire God's will?*
☐ *Has God given you the natural resources and raw material for your vision?*
☐ *Is the vision familiar to you in some way? Have you always known some form of the vision?*
☐ *Is the vision something that seems to have a home in your heart and you can't get rid of it for long?*
☐ *Is God opening some doors and arranging some opportunities for you?*
☐ *Is the vision being confirmed in the body of Christ?*

This is not an exhaustive list, but these will be a good anchor point as you let the Spirit remind you and show you indications throughout your life that God has put this vision in you.

Questions for Discussion

1. Go through the questions on the checklist and answer them in detail.

FAITH:
THE FINISH

Chapter Fourteen

THE FINISHING TOUCH

Looking unto Jesus, the author and finisher of our faith.

—Hebrews 12:2*a* KJV

Faith in its finished form results in the power and provision of God manifested in the circumstances of earth. The perfecting and finishing of our faith is accomplished through difficulties and challenges of life. As we face challenges, they train us in the ways of faith, train us to keep our focus on the reality instead of the shadow, and circumcise all the flesh out of the vision God has given us. Like muscles in the physical body, faith grows by resistance training—by being forced to do heavy lifting.

"Consider it pure joy, my brothers, whenever you face trials of many kinds, because you know that the testing of your faith develops perseverance. Perseverance must *finish its work* so that you may be mature and complete, not lacking anything" (James 1:2–4).

Difficulty becomes blessing. Trials become joy. "Sweet are the uses of adversity" (Shakespeare, *As You Like It* 2.1).

Circumcising the Vision

When God impregnates you with promise and makes vision grow in you, that vision is designed and tailored to fit you and only you. It fits you exactly. When God describes His will, He uses three words: good, pleasing, and perfect (Romans 12:2). The word "perfect" means "a perfect fit." His will for you is beneficial to you (good); it will bring you pleasure and will please you (pleasing); and it will fit you to down to the last detail (perfect). You love the vision. You're supposed to.

As the vision develops, the time comes when you are forced to recognize that although the vision is God's, it has some of your flesh wrapped around it. When I say "flesh," I am talking about those parts of your life that are still fueled by your human nature. Your flesh wants to own and control and possess and manage and manipulate. God is always working in you to free you of your flesh and move you more and more into the power of the Spirit. To that end, He arranges crisis moments at which you are brought face-to-face with your flesh and the claim it is trying to have on God's vision. Those times are painful, but they are the most productive times of all.

Moses' Parents

The writer of Hebrews spotlighted Moses' parents as prime examples of how faith works. The vision that God put into Moses began as a vision in the minds of his parents who *saw* that he was no ordinary child. God caused them to see His promise, and it jumped up and took such possession of them that a bold and reckless faith was born, freeing them from fear of the pharaoh. They didn't know all its ramifications, but their vision was that the baby would live and not die at the pharaoh's hands. That may be as far as they could see, but it was far enough.

God had to have provided supernatural protection for the baby Moses. He gave wisdom and ideas to Moses' parents. Why did they even think that a little ark of bulrushes might protect Moses' life? How did the idea even occur to them?

Three months they loved him and nurtured him and memorized his darling face and recorded in their hearts his dear sighs and gurgles and cries. With each passing day, love grew.

When the day came to let him go, imagine his mother's walk from her home to the Nile's edge. Three-month-old son entombed in a basket.

Surely only her selfless love for her son could induce her to walk her Via Dolorosa. Had she given one thought to her own desires, she would have turned back. She was going to place him into the Nile in the days when the Nile ran red with the blood of Hebrew sons. She was letting him go into the river that his enemy had declared to be his burial place. Imagine as she stood in the Nile's waters and came to that moment when she had to do the hardest thing she would ever be called upon to do. She had to let him go. She had to die to her mother's instincts to guard and protect. To save his life, she had to let him go.

When she did, her son was put upon the course he had been ordained to travel. The very river that might have been his end was instead his beginning. Jochebed received him back again, but everything had changed. When she put him into the Nile he was a slave. When she received him back from the Nile, he was a prince.

The secret was in the letting go.

Moses

Recall that Moses was among the most powerful men in Egypt— mighty in both word and action; positioned to rule Egypt; strong, handsome, intelligent, and highly educated. Moses had it all.

Moses was also pregnant with promise. An inner vision kept seeping into his thinking and his passions and grew stronger with each passing year. He wanted his Hebrew kinsmen to be free. As the vision gestated and grew more substantive, Moses realized that he wanted to be the one to free them. Then came the day when Moses tried to give birth to the vision prematurely. He tried to induce labor. He murdered an Egyptian taskmaster who was beating a Hebrew slave. At best—if all had gone well—Moses would have temporarily rescued one lone Hebrew. Do you see how far short that falls of the vision that God had in mind? Do you see what a cheap imitation we produce when the vision gets tangled up with our flesh?

When Moses happened upon this incident, he must have thought, "This is my chance. It's now or never. When I strike this blow, all my Hebrew kinsmen will recognize that I can set them free." Notice how Stephen reports it in Acts 7:25. "Moses thought that his own people would realize that God was using him to rescue them, but they did not."

Moses had no doubts about his ability to rescue Israel. He had no doubt that not only could he accomplish it, but also that the people would recognize and embrace him as their rescuer. As the vision grew in Moses until he recognized it and welcomed it, he probably thought, "Of course God has chosen and appointed me to rescue Israel. Who else? I'm the only one who could accomplish it. Anyone can see that I am the man." Moses was absolutely confident in Moses. Moses trusted in Moses.

Then Moses experienced something that he'd never experienced before in his life: failure and humiliation. He was doing what God had, from all eternity, set him in place to do. But he was doing it in his flesh.

This incident in Moses' life was all part of God's plan for how the vision would develop. Moses' failure was not a setback, but was a step forward in the gestation of the vision. Even our failures, when surrendered to the purposes of God, turn out to be essential to the development of the promise. Because of his failure, Moses' life was open to God for a new work. Now, God could take Moses' strength and make it weakness, so that He could take Moses' weakness and make it strength. When we are weak, then we are strong.

When God came to Moses 40 years later and called him to rescue Israel, the Moses who once thought that it should be obvious to anyone that he was the rescuer no longer lived. A new Moses had been born. This Moses said, "'Who am I, that I should go to Pharaoh and bring the Israelites out of Egypt?' And God said, 'I will be with you'" (Exodus 3:11–12a). From that moment, the exodus event emphasizes not who Moses is, but who God is.

God implanted the promise in Moses from his birth. He formed Moses and timed his appearance on earth for just this purpose. He grew and nourished the vision in Moses. And then He circumcised the vision. He cut away all of Moses' flesh from the promise and left it with nothing but God.

Abraham

Earlier, we looked at Abraham's faith described in the Book of Hebrews. To see this principle of circumcising the vision, we need to look at the account in the Book of Genesis and then the commentary on the story in the Book of Hebrews. (I developed this concept in my book *Legacy of Prayer* as a principle of how to put our children on God's altar. The principle also clearly applies to our concept of the vision God has given us.)

The story begins, "God tested Abraham. He said to him, 'Abraham!' 'Here I am,' he replied. Then God said, 'Take your son, your only son, Isaac, whom you love, and go to the region of Moriah. Sacrifice him there as a burnt offering on one of the mountains I will tell you about.' Early the next morning Abraham got up and saddled his donkey" (Genesis 22:1–3*a*).

God tested Abraham. The word "test" is better translated "proved." When God tests, He is not trying to discover what is inside us. He knows what is inside us. He is *proving* what is inside us. He is bringing what is inside to the outside. Don't think of this as a "trick" on God's part. He is not trying to trip Abraham up; He is proving to Abraham what God knows is in him, and He is using this crisis moment to free Abraham of his flesh. In the Book of Hebrews, we have an explanation of God's dealing with Abraham.

"By faith Abraham, when God tested him, offered Isaac as a sacrifice. He who had received the promises was about to sacrifice his one and only son, even though God had said to him, 'It is through Isaac that your offspring will be reckoned.' Abraham reasoned that God could raise the dead, and figuratively speaking, he did receive Isaac back from death" (Hebrews 11:17–19).

You remember the story. Just as Abraham was about to plunge the knife into Isaac, the Lord stopped him. Yet the writer of Hebrews says, "Abraham offered Isaac." He uses a verb tense that indicates a completed action. In the *Amplified Bible* it is translated like this: "Abraham completed the offering of Isaac." Didn't Abraham stop short of completing the offering? Yet the Bible says that he offered Isaac, completing the sacrifice. When did Abraham complete the offering of Isaac?

Go back to the account in Genesis. In the abbreviated version, God called Abraham to offer Isaac as a sacrifice, and the next morning Abraham got up and saddled his donkey for the trip. But between God's call and Abraham's obedience lay a long, dark night of struggle. You and I are left to imagine how intense that struggle must have been. We can guess at the agony through which Abraham passed. Our hearts hear Abraham crying out something like this: "If You would, let this cup pass from me!" And before the morning broke, we hear him just as clearly say, "Nevertheless, not my will, but Yours be done." It was in that dark night that Abraham completed the offering of Isaac. It was there that God received what He was asking for. How do I know that?

One of the layers of meaning in this account is that it is a picture of the crucifixion. Follow the timeline with me. Abraham got up, saddled his donkey, and set out for the place God would show Him (Genesis 22:2–3). He traveled for *three days* (Genesis 22:4), then took Isaac to the top of the mountain and prepared to sacrifice him on the altar. Instead of killing Isaac, God stopped him and Abraham received Isaac back in a resurrection: "and figuratively speaking, he did receive Isaac back from death" (Hebrews 11:19). If Abraham traveled for three days and on the third day received Isaac back in a type of resurrection, then when did Isaac die? The sacrifice was completed on the long, agonizing night that brought about Abraham's yielded obedience. Three days later, Abraham received Isaac back in a resurrection.

God considered the sacrifice to be completed. God got what He was after. What was God wanting from Abraham? What was the sacrifice?

Abraham was connected to Isaac in two ways. First, Isaac was the son of his flesh. He was to Abraham "your son, your only son, Isaac, whom you love" (Genesis 22:2). You can imagine how very strong that connection was. After having waited and yearned for this son until all rational hope was gone and his and Sarah's bodies were long past child-bearing years, at last Isaac was born. As his son, in the days of Abraham, Isaac was his property. He had the right to do with him as he chose. You know that every choice Abraham made concerning Isaac was made out of an overflow of love.

Abraham was connected to Isaac in another way. Isaac was also the child of promise, born by the power of the Spirit (Galatians 4:28–29). It was through Isaac that all of the promise of God—that which had defined Abraham's entire adult life—was to be realized. "He who had received the promises was about to sacrifice his one and only son, *even though God had said* to him, 'It is through Isaac that your offspring will be reckoned' (Hebrews 11:17*b*–18). Abraham was connected to Isaac spiritually. Isaac was to Abraham both the child of his flesh and the child of the promise.

On the night that Abraham completed the offering, Isaac did not die to Abraham, but Abraham died to his flesh connection with Isaac. He let his father-flesh die. He relinquished ownership. That was the night he laid Isaac on the altar. It was Abraham's crucifixion, not Isaac's.

In requiring Abraham to die to his flesh connection, God did not require Abraham to die to the spiritual promise. Abraham, I believe, was more alive than ever to the promise in Isaac. As he reached the place of the sacrifice, "he said to his servants, 'Stay here with the donkey while I and the boy go over there. *We will worship* and then *we will come back to you*'" (Genesis 22:5). The writer of Hebrews says, "Abraham reasoned that God could raise the dead, and figuratively speaking, he did receive Isaac back from death" (Hebrews 11:19). By the time he had become fully yielded to the voice of God, by the time he had dealt the death-blow to his own flesh, he had reached a new level of faith in God. He was absolutely certain that, no matter what path the promise took, the promise of God would not fail.

Mary

Imagine Mary as she stood at the foot of the cross, watching the last drop of life drain from the body of her son. Surely she remembered the visit from the angel of the Lord as if it were only yesterday, when he announced to her that she would give birth to the Promise.

Mary, as she stood watching the Promise die, did not know about the resurrection. As she watched the Promise shed His blood on the altar, she didn't understand that by losing Him, she would be gaining Him for all eternity. By giving up her son, she received her Savior.

Circumcising Your Vision

Your overall life vision and the mini-visions along the way all will go through a circumcision when your flesh will have to die. You will have to relinquish ownership. You will have to let it go and lay it down, knowing that only if God gives it back in resurrection form will it live. The vision cannot be born until your flesh has been cut away.

When Abraham's promise was about to be born, the last rite that God demanded of him was the covenant of circumcision. Before the vision could be born, Abraham's flesh had to be cut off. Let me say this as delicately as possible. The very part of Abram's body from which Isaac will receive life must be circumcised of flesh. Isaac must come from the "covenant in [Abram's] flesh" (Genesis 17:13). Jesus said, "Flesh gives birth to flesh, but the Spirit gives birth to spirit" (John 3:6).

When the nation of Israel responded to the promise of God in their flesh—when they refused to enter the Promised Land because they were fueled by fear—God declared that none of that generation would enter the land. Flesh cannot inherit the promise. Flesh cannot function in the realm of faith. When that generation of flesh had died, then the people could enter the land. Notice what had to happen as soon as they crossed over and set up camp in the land. Before they could occupy the land and subdue their enemies, God commanded Joshua to circumcise them. No one had been circumcised in the desert while they wandered in the land of their flesh. But nothing could go forward in the Promised Land until all flesh had been circumcised.

> *Now this is why he did so: All those who came out of Egypt—all the men of military age—died in the desert on the way after leaving Egypt. All the people that came out had been circumcised, but all the people born in the desert during the journey from Egypt had not. The Israelites had moved about in the desert forty years until all the men who were of military age when they left Egypt had died, since they had not obeyed the LORD. For the LORD had sworn to them that they would not see the land that he had solemnly promised their fathers to give us, a land flowing with milk and honey. So he raised up their sons in their place, and these were the ones Joshua circumcised. They were still uncircumcised because they had not been circumcised on the way. And after the whole nation had been circumcised, they remained where they were in camp until they were healed.*
>
> —Joshua 5:4–8

When you come to that moment, don't resist it. Recognize it for what it is. Walk away and leave it on the altar. Don't try to put it on life support. Don't try to resuscitate it. If it is God's vision, He will give it back to you in its resurrection form. Your job is to hand your flesh over to be crucified.

Questions for Discussion

1. Identify times in your life when God has brought you to a moment where the vision had to be circumcised of flesh.

2. What has God been speaking to you about in this chapter on letting your flesh connection die?

3. Where are you resisting God's crucifying work in the vision He has given you?

Chapter Fifteen

THE PROCESS OF PURITY

Who can bring what is pure from the impure?

—Job 14:4

G od is purifying you so that which He brings forth from you will be pure. He is working in you a process that goes beyond simple obedience to the roots of unrighteousness that produce disobedience. He is cleansing you moment by moment, moving you from one level to the next, and never leaving you to "sit on your dregs."

> *Moab has been at ease since his youth; he has also been undisturbed, like wine on its dregs, and he has not been emptied from vessel to vessel, nor has he gone into exile. Therefore he retains his flavor, and his aroma has not changed.*
>
> —Jeremiah 48:11 NASB

God says that Moab has been left undisturbed. He is describing what a person is like who has never been challenged and forced to face disappointment or disruption of his life. He is like wine on its dregs. Wine left to sit on its dregs becomes bitter and harsh. It is unpalatable. It is useless.

The art of winemaking involves stages. A wine must be moved from vessel to vessel along the way. Each stage of winemaking requires a vessel of different size, shape, and construction. Each stage accomplishes something different for the final product—the wine that is becoming. At each stage, the dregs have settled to the bottom and must be strained out to prevent the ruin of the wine. The stage at which a wine must be emptied from one vessel to another is not a static and predictable period. Only the winemaker can tell.

God, the Great Winemaker, is fermenting a rich and perfect wine in you. Do you feel yourself being emptied from vessel to vessel? You get used to the shape and feel of your life, and then you find yourself being emptied out. During part of the process, you have been poured out, but not poured in yet. You know that your old vessel has been emptied out, but you do not feel yourself having arrived in a new vessel yet. There is a transition period, a pouring. It is disorienting and uncertain. Then you find yourself poured into a life of a completely different shape and size made up of new materials. It is new to you, and it doesn't feel like it fits.

Learn the ways of the Winemaker. Don't be discouraged or frightened when the shape of your life and the construction of your days seem to be changing. God will not let you sit on your dregs. Unlike Moab, you will not stay in the same place. You will not be locked into your immaturity, retaining the same aroma as in your youth. He is ripening you, fermenting you, enriching you.

Rejoice! You are being emptied from vessel to vessel. At each new stage your dregs are being filtered out.

Sometimes you are in a vessel long enough to get very used to it, and when you are poured out of that vessel, you feel that you have lost your focus or that your commitment has waned. Maybe God wants to show you that you have come to trust in the forms of your faith instead of in God. You have leaned on the expressions of your faith instead of in the object of your faith.

Anytime you are poured from vessel to vessel, it is for your benefit, not your harm.

When He invites us to come reason with Him, He then tells us where that reasoning will point. He invites us to come reason with Him, and then tells us the most unreasonable concept of all. "'Come now, let us reason together,' says the LORD. 'Though your sins are like scarlet, they shall be as white as snow; though they are red as crimson, they shall be like wool'" (Isaiah 1:18).

He does not call you to account in order to convict you and condemn you to punishment, but to cleanse you and restore you to life.

Faith is how the power of God gets into the circumstances of earth. Power flows from purity. "If you remain in me and my words remain in you, ask whatever you wish and it will be given you" (John 15:7).

(1) "If you remain in me and my words remain in you": **the process of purity**

(2) "ask whatever you wish and it will be given you": **the promise of power**

Notice that the process of purity precedes the promise of power. Don't seek power. Seek purity.

Launderer's Soap

"Who can endure the day of his coming? Who can stand when he appears? For he will be like a refiner's fire or a launderer's soap. He will sit as a refiner and purifier of silver" (Malachi 3:2–3).

When the Messiah enters your life, He will do so with power—refining and washing and purifying. His Word living in you, freely occupying every corner or your life, is washing you clean. When His Word is at home in you, what does it accomplish? It cleanses and purifies. "You are already clean because of the word I have spoken to you" (John 15:3).

His Word is acting as His detergent. Lather, rinse, and repeat. Keep taking it in, letting Him speak it to you in His living voice.

Circumstances are another of His detergents. "For our light and momentary troubles are achieving for us an eternal glory that far outweighs them all" (2 Corinthians 4:17). You have seen that He is using circumstances and people in your life to produce an eternal weight of glory. They are washing you clean, if you let them. As you pass through difficult circumstances—daily irritations or devastating events—keep your eyes focused, not on what you can see, but on what you can't see.

Consider Jesus. We have dissected the eleventh chapter of Hebrews to see what God wants to teach us about faith. Let's read where we go from there: "Therefore, since we are surrounded by such a great cloud of witnesses, let us throw off everything that hinders and the sin that so easily entangles, and let us run with perseverance the race marked out for us. Let us fix our eyes on Jesus, the author and perfecter of our faith, who for the joy set before him endured the cross, scorning its shame, and sat down at the right hand of the throne of God" (Hebrews 12:1–2).

> *Look away from everything else and be transfixed by Jesus.*

The writer of Hebrews has just laid out for us a list of individuals whose lives bore witness to the power of faith. When he says that we are surrounded by a cloud of witnesses, he does not mean that they are looking at us, but that we are looking at them. But that is not where our gaze should rest. Let us *fix our eyes* on Jesus. The Greek word translated "fix our eyes" means "to stare at, to be transfixed by." It has a prefix that means "away, or off." Look away from everything else and be transfixed by Jesus. He is the one who is authoring our faith. He is the one who is perfecting our faith. Glance at all the other witnesses, but let your gaze come to rest on Jesus.

"Who for the joy set before him endured the cross, scorning its shame" (Hebrews 12:2*b*). Kenneth S. Wuest, Greek scholar, says that this word "for" (*anti*) means "in exchange for" or "instead of." He points to Luke 11:11 as an example of its use. "Which of you fathers, if your son asks for a fish, will give him a snake instead (*anti*)?" The word translated "set before" means literally "lying before." He thinks that this sentence is saying that Jesus, instead of choosing to hold onto His rightful place in the presence of the Father—the joy laid out in front of Him—chose instead the cross and its shame. Greek scholar Marvin R. Vincent concurs, saying, "The joy was the full, divine beatitude of his preincarnate life in the bosom of the Father; the glory which he had with God before the world was. In exchange for this he accepted the cross and the shame" (M.R. Vincent, *Vincent's Word Studies in the New Testament*).

This aligns with what the author had just spoken of Moses: "He regarded disgrace for the sake of Christ as of greater value than the treasures of Egypt, because he was looking ahead to his reward" (Hebrews 11:26).

When we fix our gaze on Jesus, we see faith in its fullest form. You and I will endure the difficulties thrust upon us, knowing them to be working an eternal weight of glory. But Jesus *chose* the cross. He saw past the circumstances to the purpose behind them. He knew the Father into whose hands He had entrusted His life and His path. He loved the Father's honor more than His own comfort. He loved me so much that, when presented with the choice between His joyful state in the bosom of the Father or the rugged cross, He chose the cross *instead of* the joy set before Him. I can't comprehend it.

He knew that the path of the cross would lead finally to resurrection. He kept His eyes on the outcome. He laid down His own life and now has received it back in its resurrection form.

Begin to speak the language of faith that says, "I choose the crucifixion of my flesh. I choose not to duck or hide from it or rationalize it. I choose to let my flesh die, and I embrace the resurrection power that will come as a result." Fix your eyes on Jesus, the author and perfecter of your faith.

Questions for Discussion

1. How is the process of purity at work in your life right now?

2. How is the Word of God acting as detergent in your life?

3. How are circumstances acting as detergent in your life?

4. What do you see when you look away from your circumstances and fix your eyes on Jesus?

Chapter Sixteen

THE PRAYER OF FAITH

Jesus replied, "I tell you the truth, if you have faith and do not doubt, not only can you do what was done to the fig tree, but also you can say to this mountain, 'Go, throw yourself into the sea,' and it will be done. If you believe, you will receive whatever you ask for in prayer."

—Matthew 21:21–22

The prayer of faith rises out of the life of faith. Prayer is the spoken expression of faith, and nothing is too big or too difficult for the power of prayer to accomplish. Jesus said that the *very same thing* He did to the fig tree (withered it with a word) was not beyond the ability of His disciples to do. We will do it the very same way He did it—by faith expressed through obedience and spoken in prayer.

The act of prayer is speaking faith. Faith comes by hearing, and hearing comes from the voice of Christ speaking to us. What we hear from Him, we speak into the situation. What we see in our Father's presence, we announce to our circumstances.

Let's examine four components of faith-fueled prayer. These four components work synergistically, meaning that one works in company with all the others to create the whole. The whole is greater than the sum of its parts. I suggest that the four components of prayer are praise, purity, petition, and pliability.

Praise

Context is everything. When you look at a landscape painting, the background is what defines the foreground. Your eye discerns the individual elements of the composite painting in terms of the background.

When you live in a flow of praise, the background against which your circumstances appear is realistic. Against the backdrop of who God is, everything else is perceived correctly.

Praise is a key element in prayer. "I will extol the LORD at all times; his praise will always be on my lips" (Psalm 34:1). Jesus, the Prayer Master, taught His disciples to pray by opening with "Our Father...hallowed be your name," and ending with, "yours is the kingdom and the power and the glory forever." All of the petitions were wrapped in praise.

Praise puts the focus where it belongs—on God. You find that as you stay God-centered rather than problem-centered, you see your circumstances from a different vantage point. You see them in terms of God's power—the power that exceeds your imagination.

> *Say to God, "How awesome are your deeds! So great is your power that your enemies cringe before you."*
>
> —Psalm 66:3

> *Great is our LORD and mighty in power; his understanding has no limit.*
>
> —Psalm 147:5

> *Praise him for his acts of power; praise him for his surpassing greatness.*
>
> —Psalm 150:2

Praise causes your mind to stay fixed on Him, "letting it swing like the needle, to the polestar of the soul" (Thomas R. Kelly, *A Testament of*

Devotion). You find that God is like a magnet, drawing your thoughts toward Him. The more you bring your life into active cooperation with Him, opening yourself to Him through praise, the more He exerts that drawing power on your heart. Praise fastens your heart on Him.

Praise creates an openness toward God and the things of God. It sensitizes you to what God is doing around you and in you. Learn to praise Him continually. You can be thanking Him for what He is doing in every situation, even as the situation unfolds. If you develop a habit of praise, you will find that you are always watching for how God is using every moment of your day. This fountain of praise will turn every situation into a theater for His activity. Little things that might have gone unnoticed take on new significance as you learn to recognize His grand, eternal purpose being worked out in incidents that seem insignificant in the moment: a chance encounter, a random conversation, one door of opportunity opens while another closes, finding yourself at the right place at the right time. When you cultivate a heart of praise, you will find adventure at every turn. You will recognize and celebrate His plan and provision as it progresses. "The lot is cast into the lap, but its every decision is from the LORD" (Proverbs 16:33). What may appear to be random or by chance is really being orchestrated by the Lord. When, through continual praise, you train yourself to watch expectantly for Him, *you will see Him.*

Praise builds faith. Praise is built on who God is. God teaches us who He is by what He does. God calls His people to praise by telling them to remember His deeds in the past.

> *I will remember the deeds of the LORD; yes, I will remember your miracles of long ago. I will meditate on all your works and consider all your mighty deeds.*
>
> —Psalm 77:11–12

I remember the days of long ago; I meditate on all your works and consider what your hands have done. I spread out my hands to you; my soul thirsts for you like a parched land.

—Psalm 143:5–6

As you remember what God has done in the past, for you and for others, it will strengthen your faith. "Summon your power, O God; show us your strength, O God, as you have done before" (Psalm 68:28). Throughout the Psalms, the people praised God as they remembered His mighty acts:

Come and see what God has done, how awesome his works in man's behalf! He turned the sea into dry land, they passed through the waters on foot—come, let us rejoice in him.

—Psalm 66:5–6

When David faced impossible odds—his slingshot against the fierce, armored, well-armed giant warrior Goliath—his faith was fed by God's past faithfulness. "The LORD who delivered me from the paw of the lion and the paw of the bear will deliver me from the hand of this Philistine" (1 Samuel 17:37).

As you begin deliberately to develop a life of praise, let the record of God's deeds build an understanding of who He is. Read the Scriptures and meditate on His power. Put yourself in position to hear from others what God does in their lives. Recall God's work in your own life. Keep a personal journal of God's activity in your life. Go back to it and let it remind you.

Praise stirs up love for God. Increased passion will be the natural outgrowth of praise. Your genuine love will be reflected to those around you. Your praise will begin to attract others to God. As you praise God, your life becomes His platform.

I will extol the LORD at all times; his praise will always be on my lips. My soul will boast in the LORD; let the afflicted hear and rejoice. Glorify the LORD with me; let us exalt his name together. I sought the LORD, and he answered me; he delivered me from all my fears. Those who look to him are radiant; their faces are never covered with shame.

—Psalm 34:1–5

Praise can change the way you view life. Sometimes praise is an offering, a sacrifice. "I will sacrifice a thank offering to you and call on the name of the LORD" (Psalm 116:17). There are times when the circumstances of your life would appear to call for anything but praise. At these times, praise may be an act of your will. Praise may be a discipline and a decision. When, in the face of difficult circumstances, you *choose* praise, you will find that your view of the circumstances changes. You choose your role as either victim or victor by how you respond in the face of difficult circumstances.

In Acts 16, we read about an incident in the life of Paul. He and Silas were publicly flogged and thrown into jail, their feet fastened in stocks. Yet they praised God. In fact, they praised God with such gusto that the other prisoners and the prison guards listened to them. How could they praise God is such devastating circumstances? Because they knew their God. They were not praising God because they knew what He was going to do. They were surprised by what He did. They could be in chains. It didn't matter. They were free no matter what. "Praise and thanksgiving do not magically change my circumstances. They radically alter my viewpoint" (Jennifer Kennedy Dean, *Heart's Cry*).

The ability to choose praise as an act of obedience in spite of your feelings comes from knowing God. When you face difficulties, disappointments, or heartaches, take inventory of what you know about God. Reason.

God is good.

For the LORD is good and his love endures forever; his faithfulness continues through all generations.

—Psalm 100:5

You are good, and what you do is good.

—Psalm 119:68*a*

Give thanks to the LORD, for he is good. His love endures forever.

—Psalm 136:1

God loves you.

But I trust in your unfailing love; my heart rejoices in your salvation.

—Psalm 13:5

For the king trusts in the Lord; through the unfailing love of the Most High he will not be shaken.

—Psalm 21:7

May your unfailing love rest upon us, O LORD, even as we put our hope in you.

—Psalm 33:22

I trust in God's unfailing love for ever and ever.

—Psalm 52:8*b*

I will declare that your love stands firm forever, that you established your faithfulness in heaven itself.

—Psalm 89:2

The LORD is gracious and compassionate, slow to anger and rich in love.

—Psalm 145:8

God is in control. He is working everything toward a good end. *According to the plan of him who works out everything in conformity with the purpose of his will.*

—Ephesians 1:11

And we know that in all things God works for the good of those who love him, who have been called according to his purpose.

—Romans 8:28

"For I know the plans I have for you," declares the LORD, "plans to prosper you and not to harm you, plans to give you hope and a future."

—Jeremiah 29:11

These truths will not change. God remains the same forever. In the midst of your circumstances, God is still who He claims to be. You can praise God for what He will bring out of your situation. You can praise Him for what He is doing in you and in others through the situation. You can praise Him because you know He has a plan. You do not have to be crushed by circumstances because you know the God who is in control of past, present, and future. Praise Him.

Begin today to develop the discipline of praise. Determine to respond to every situation today by praising God. Commit to meditating on the power, the character, and the mighty deeds of God, turning those thoughts into praise. Ask the Spirit to remind you and to teach you.

Purity

Praise leads naturally to an awareness of sin in your life. Having fixed the eyes of your heart on Him, your own sin-tattered life comes more clearly into focus.

True and authentic prayer is based on a two-fold revelation: the revelation of who God is and the revelation of who I am.

Remember Isaiah? He saw the Lord, high and exalted. He saw the glory and the holiness. Instinctively he cried out: "Woe to me!...I am ruined! For I am a man of unclean lips, and I live among a people of unclean lips, and my eyes have seen the King, the LORD Almighty" (Isaiah 6:5). And Job? "'My ears had heard of you but now my eyes have seen you. Therefore I despise myself and repent in dust and ashes'" (Job 42:5–6).

His holiness exposes your sinfulness. His strength reveals your weakness. His faithfulness lays bare your faithlessness. Only in the light of His presence can we see the truth about ourselves. "In your light we see light" (Psalm 36:9*b*). "Everything exposed by the light becomes visible, for it is light that makes everything visible" (Ephesians 5:13–14*a*).

Until you have a true picture of yourself, you will be unable to enter into the depths of the kingdom. You will be incapable of experiencing genuine prayer. The stark contrast between the Holy One in His splendor and me in my filthy rags—the revelation of His worthiness and my unworthiness—compels me to fall on my face in awe. You see, the awe comes not only from His majesty, but from the fact that He seeks *me* out; that He delights in *me*; that He loves *my* presence. Me! In all my weakness, in all my failure, and in all my sin, His bloodstained love reaches out and draws me into His presence.

Jesus taught His disciples that purity was vital to a praying life. Jesus showed them that the Father's love for them was so great that He was unwilling to leave them in their sin. He desires relationship with you so much that He not only paid the penalty for your sins Himself, but He continues to move in your life to remove sinful behaviors. You are of such great worth to Him that He keeps seeking you out and drawing you to His heart.

God hates what sin does to you. He hates sin because it diminishes you and harms you. He calls you to repentance because He loves you. As He becomes your focus, you begin to see sin the same way He does. You want to be clean before Him.

God hates sin because it diminishes you and harms you. He calls you to repentance because He loves you.

"Repent, then, and turn to God, so that your sins may be wiped out, that times of refreshing may come from the Lord" (Acts 3:19).

To repent means to change directions. It means to turn around. Make a u-turn. It means to walk away from the old thing and walk purposefully toward the new thing. In order to repent, not only must you understand what you are walking away from, but you must also understand what you are walking toward. The Holy Spirit, whose job it is to convict you of sin and unrighteousness (John 16:8–9), will convict you of *specific* sins. His conviction will not be general or generic. He won't say, "You're so awful. You can't get it right." He'll say, "You just told a lie. You need to go back immediately and tell the truth." Here's what happens: as you continue to repent when the Spirit convicts you, soon that holy habit will begin to keep you from sinning in the first place. You might say to yourself as you are about to tell a lie, "If I tell this lie, I'll just have to come back and tell the truth later. I might as well tell the truth now."

Also, as your relationship with the Lord increases in intimacy and you learn to delight in Him, you are unwilling for anything to come between you. You don't want to grieve Him. You begin to love Him more than you love your sin. You recognize the Spirit's conviction as the love of God. He is determined that you, His beloved, will not be cheated out of the full measure of intimacy by making a compromise with sin.

Your relationship with God is more intimate than a marriage. He says that our relationship to Him is closer than the relationship between husband and wife. While man and woman become "one flesh" through marriage, "he who unites himself with the Lord is one with him in spirit" (1 Corinthians 6:17). When we flirt with sin, God calls it adultery.

When we deliberately choose sin over Him, we are aligning ourselves with His enemy. We are being unfaithful to His love. We are committing adultery! "You adulterous people, don't you know that friendship with the world is hatred toward God?" (James 4:4a).

Deliberate, willful sin creates a barrier between you and God. No matter what your lips say, by continuing in sin with an unrepentant heart, your actions say that your heart is not His. Your actions say that your sin means more to you than intimacy with God. "The LORD says: 'These people come near to me with their mouth and honor me with their lips, but their hearts are far from me'" (Isaiah 29:13a).

> Sin is an awful thing. One of the most awful things about it is the way it hinders prayer. It severs the connections between us and the source of all grace and power and blessing. Anyone who desires power in prayer must be merciless in dealing with his own sins. "If I regard iniquity in my heart, the Lord will not hear me" (Psalm 66:18 KJV). As long as we hold on to sin or have any controversy with God, we cannot expect Him to heed our prayers. If there is anything that is constantly coming up in your moments of close communion with God, that is the thing that hinders prayer. Put it away.
>
> —R.A. Torrey, *How to Pray*

If you would have all of God, He must have all of you. He will not share you with another. He will not be satisfied with words of love. He wants to be the sole possessor of your heart. He wants to reign in you as your King and Lord. Your heart was made for Him. Only as you walk away from sin and into His waiting arms do you discover your destiny. It is His love for you that motivates Him to search your heart and pinpoint sin. Respond to that love. Respond quickly to anything about which the Spirit is convicting you. Turn your back on your sin.

Search me, O God, and know my heart; test me and know my anxious thoughts. See if there is any offensive way in me, and lead me in the way everlasting.

—Psalm 139:23–24

Create in me a pure heart, O God, and renew a steadfast spirit within me.

—Psalm 51:10.

Petition

Because of His desire to have an intimate relationship with us, God has designed prayer. He has chosen to allow us to be involved with Him as He demonstrates His power and His provision on the earth. When we discover the direct link between our requests and His answers, our love for Him increases, our worship of Him deepens, and our desire to be in right relationship with Him grows. He wants us to ask Him for everything we need because He wants us to learn by experience that He is our provider. He wants us to know for ourselves that we can trust Him. Hannah Hurnard says, "It helps us to utter dependence upon God and gives Him the opportunity to confirm our trust in Him and experience His grace in a way which would be absolutely impossible otherwise. He has got everything ready and planned in order to meet all our needs before we ever realize what they are. But in order to teach us this joy of utter dependence and trust, He waits for us to ask" (Hannah Hurnard, *Hearing Heart*).

If you remain in me and my words remain in you, ask whatever you wish, and it will be given you.

—John 15:7

Our asking begins with our intimate relationship with Him. Jesus says that when we are remaining in Him, then our prayers will be "powerful and effective" (James 5:16). When His words are in residence in our lives, then our prayers consistently will have power. He will be able to transform your mind from the inside, and you will find yourself asking for those things that line up with His will. Oswald Chambers says, "Prayer is...the means whereby we assimilate more and more of His mind" (Oswald Chambers, *Christian Disciplines*).

What can you do to be sure that you are remaining in Him? Jesus gives two clues in John 15. He first says that when you remain in Him, His words are remaining in you (John 15:7). Stay in His Word. Read it, study it, memorize it, meditate on it, listen to it, talk about it. Let His Word come to life in you. His Word will renew your mind so that your life is proof of His power (Romans 12:2). You will know how to pray as you let His Word, like a two-edged sword, divide soul from spirit (Hebrews 4:12).

The second clue Jesus gives for how to remain in Him is found in John 15:10. "If you obey my commands, you will remain in my love, just as I have obeyed my Father's commands and remain in his love." As you obey Him moment by moment, you find your intimacy with Him growing and your power in prayer increasing. Your obedience progressively synchronizes your heart and His. You find your thoughts more and more in tune with His. "The goal of a praying life is His desires poured into my heart so they become my desires and are expressed through my prayers" (Jennifer Kennedy Dean, *Live a Praying Life*).

Asking, then, grows out of relationship. Asking is simply opening our lives to His abundance. O. Hallesby says, "To pray is to let Jesus glorify his name in the midst of our needs....To pray is nothing more involved than to open the door, giving Jesus access to our needs and permitting Him to exercise His own power in dealing with them" (O. Hallesby, *Prayer*).

Jim Weidmann, vice chairman of the National Day of Prayer Task Force, describes asking like this: his dad was an engineer in whose skills Jim had utter confidence. Often, as a boy, Jim and his buddies would ride their bikes over terrain that was not bike-friendly. When a friend's bike would be damaged, Jim would say the most logical thing he could think of. "Let's take it to my dad." Jim says, "I thought of it like this. Your bike's broken. Let's take it to the best engineer I know. That's all we needed to know—where to take it." As you live in daily intimacy with Jesus, you will have that same kind of spontaneous confidence in Him. You won't have to be concerned about the size of the problem or the extent of the damage. All you need to know is where to take it.

All the elements of prayer are blending into a whole. **Praise** encourages us to **ask** because it reminds us of God's great power and love. **Repentance** clears our lives of those things that hinder intimacy, opening the way for us to live in unity with Him, **asking** for the things He longs to give. **Asking** leads us to more **praise** as we experience His work in the world through our prayers. The adventure of **asking** and receiving compels us to **turn away from sin** so that we can walk in even more of His magnificent power.

What is it that you need? Ask Him.

Pliability

As these first three elements of prayer take root, the natural outgrowth is a yielded, surrendered life. Our lives are becoming more pliable in His hands. The Master Potter is shaping us into His image. He teaches us to pray the prayer of the pliable life: "Let your will be done on earth as it is in heaven."

This prayer, once you have learned to pray it from the depths of your heart, can begin to fill your whole life. For prayer not only has power with God in heaven, it also affects our hearts....The will of God is the center of the universe, the pivot about which all things revolve and which upholds all. Earnest prayer makes the will of God central in our hearts; it upholds and directs us; it renews and glorifies us, making us pleasing to Him.

O Christian, have you already chosen the will of God as your portion, your treasure, your delight? If not…learn how to pray this prayer in such a way that God can give you the complete answer; His will within you now, on earth, as in heaven. Begin today to let His will take possession of your heart. God wills to give Himself to you. By way of His will, God and heaven enter your heart; allow God and His will to fill it. Doing His will from the heart will make your life a heavenly life.

—Andrew Murray, *Not My Will*

The most freeing discovery you will ever make is that God's will for you fits you. Yielding all of your life to Him, though difficult and even painful in the moment, is the only way to find true satisfaction and complete fulfillment. A pliable and surrendered life will produce powerful prayer.

The first aspect of a pliable heart is that it is entirely surrendered to God in the daily living out of His will.

There is a way chosen for you. "Who, then, is the man that fears the LORD? He will instruct him in the way chosen for him" (Psalm 25:12). God has a specific plan for you, and as you trust and follow Him, the plan unfolds. His will for you, His design for your life, fits you in every way. It is not a generic, off-the-rack plan that would fit just anyone. He has designed a life just for you. As you surrender to Him, you do not lose yourself; you find yourself. As you obey Him step by step, a steadfast peace settles on you. Your heart cries, "My food is to do the will of the one who sent me!" His will satisfies your deepest yearnings, nourishes your soul, strengthens you. His will is all you need and all you desire.

—Jennifer Kennedy Dean, *He Leads Me Beside Still Waters*

As you find yourself fully engaged in a *life* of prayer, doing God's specific will, living His carefully crafted plan for your life, it becomes natural that your prayers most often reflect His will. Obedience—surrendering to His commands—keeps you in a position where His life can flow through you like the vine's life flows through the branch.

As you carry on in your life of yielded obedience, you see that your repentance from particular sins leads you into deeper surrender. A pliable life has taken repentance to the next level. You have come to love the presence of the Lord as you develop a life of praise. The more you love the Lord's presence, the more you hate sin. The more you hate sin, the more likely you are to turn away from it before you act. "The prudent see danger and take refuge, but the simple keep going and suffer for it" (Proverbs 27:12). "But put on the Lord Jesus Christ, and make no provision for the flesh in regard to its lusts" (Romans 13:14 NASB). As you are surrendered to Him and obedient to

In yielding your prayer to His will, you will find that His plan exceeds your imagination.

Him, you find yourself dealing with sin *before* you commit it. Little by little, you learn to respond to the pull of righteousness instead of responding to the pull of sin. Now you are developing both clean hands (right behavior) and a pure heart (right motives). "Who may ascend the hill of the LORD? Who may stand in his holy place? He who has clean hands and a pure heart" (Psalm 24:3–4a).

The second aspect of a pliable life is that the content of your prayers begins to reflect your surrender. "Not my will, but Your will be done in this situation." In yielding your prayer to His will, you will find that His plan exceeds your imagination. Denise Glenn, founder of MotherWise and author of numerous books on mothering, tells how her most difficult surrender was the open door for her most fulfilling life.

> As a tiny girl, I wanted to be a mother. Baby dolls were my constant companions. The Christmas I was 14, my mother told me that it was

the last Christmas I would get a doll—it was getting embarrassing!

My love for babies never left me. After David Glenn and I married while attending Texas Tech University, I patiently waited through graduation and the purchase of our first little house to begin a family. However, God had other plans.

Infertility plagued us, and I finally consulted a Christian counselor for help in dealing with the pain. My counselor suggested what sounded like a simple solution: "Tell God it's okay if you never have a child; what you want is Him." Thinking I could complete any "Christian" assignment, I walked out of the office and tried to pray that prayer. However, it occurred to me that God might take me up on it! For three days and nights I wrestled with the Lord. I finally got on my face on my shag carpet (this was 1975 and you could literally hang on to your carpet!) and told God it was okay if I never had a child, what I wanted was Him—and I wasn't even sure what that meant! I was immediately at peace and assumed that meant that God had heard my prayer and that we would not have children.

God must have been smiling. Soon those little dolls of my childhood were replaced with three little girls—all born within four years. Being a mother had finally become a reality. But it wasn't quite the fantasy world I had imagined. Overwhelmed with three preschoolers, I began a diligent search to discover how to be a better mom.

—Denise Glenn, *Freedom for Mothers*

From that painful surrender, Denise's powerful ministry, MotherWise, was born. Moments of full surrender may indeed be difficult. But they will cause your life to be totally open to God's greater plan. At those moments of surrender, you have the privilege of deliberately taking hold of that for which Christ Jesus took hold of you (Philippians 3:12), even when that means letting go of what you think is best.

A pliable heart, a heart that is like soft, moldable clay in the hands of the Master Potter, yields a life of peace and power.

Praise, purity, petition, pliability—the elements that come together to form the mightiest force in the world: PRAYER.

Questions for Discussion

1. What circumstance in your life do you most resent or fear?

2. Would you deliberately praise God for what He is doing in that circumstance that He could not do without it?

3. What sin in your life is God bringing to your attention?

4. Would you right now acknowledge the harmful effect that sin has in your life and ask God to exercise all His power on your behalf to set you free?

5. What do you want to ask God for right now?

6. Where do you need to yield your desires to God?

Chapter Seventeen

PRAYER POINTS

I invite you now on a 52-week odyssey of praying and opening your life to God's voice and to His present-tense, at-hand power. One of the challenges about the discipline of praying is the tendency to fall into a rut. In the following pages, I suggest 52 ways of praying actively. Maybe your family, your prayer group, or your church would like to take this journey together. Meet together weekly to discuss and share the week's experience and encourage one another and join your voices in agreement with the Word of God. Happy traveling!

52 Prayer Points
By Jennifer Kennedy Dean

1. "The king's heart is in the hand of the LORD; he directs it like a watercourse wherever he pleases" (Proverbs 21:1).

If your thoughts wander during your prayer time, instead of trying to force them back into your pre-set agenda, try following them. Perhaps the Lord has another agenda.

2. "But when you pray, go into your room, close the door and pray to your Father, who is unseen" (Matthew 6:6*a*).

Set a time for daily prayer. Consider it an unbreakable commitment. Keep your set appointment every day for one week. For one solid week, let your scheduled prayer time be the centerpiece of your day; arrange everything else to fit around it.

3. "Very early in the morning, while it was still dark, Jesus got up, left the house and went off to a solitary place, where he prayed" (Mark 1:35).

Give God the first fruits of your day. For one week, give the very first 30 minutes of your day to prayer.

4. "But Jesus often withdrew to lonely places and prayed" (Luke 5:16).

Find a place in your home where you can be alone and undistracted during your prayer time. Keep your Bible, your prayer journal, a pen, and whatever tools you use in that place so that everything is ready. During your prayer time each day, this is a sacred place.

5. "I saw the LORD seated on a throne, high and exalted, and the train of his robe filled the temple" (Isaiah 6:1).

As you start your prayer time, before you say anything, let your mind's eye see Him, high and exalted, and yourself in a position of worship before Him. Stay in that inner posture until His glory fills your thoughts as the train of His robe fills the temple.

6. "But Jesus said, 'Someone touched me; I know that power has gone out from me'" (Luke 8:46).

Take time to become truly alive to His presence with you. Be aware that as you touch Him through prayer, His power is released into your life.

7. "O my people, hear my teaching; listen to the words of my mouth" (Psalm 78:1).

Read your Bible this morning with the awareness that you are listening to the words of His mouth. Stop at the first word, phrase, or thought that captures your attention and let the Father speak to you about it and let it shape your prayers.

8. "We are the clay, you are the potter; we are all the work of your hand" (Isaiah 64:8*b*).

This week, practice the prayer of pliability. Instead of focusing on what you want God to do for you, focus on allowing Him to shape your desires until they match His. Accept each situation in your life as His hand shaping your thoughts, character, and longings.

9. "Not my will, but yours be done" (Luke 22:42*b*).

This week, let these words be the only prayer you pray about situations that confront you. Focus on relinquishing every situation to Him to be a platform for His power.

10. "I will remember the deeds of the LORD" (Psalm 77:11*a*).

This week, try writing out your prayers. It will help you stay focused and will create a record of God's work in your life.

11. "My tongue will speak of your righteousness and of your praises all day long" (Psalm 35:28).

This week, pray aloud during your prayer time. It will make your prayer experience more concrete and help keep your mind focused.

12. "Fix these words of mine in your hearts and minds...talking about them when you sit at home and when you walk along the road, when you lie down and when you get up" (Deuteronomy 11:18–19).

This week, try walking as you pray. Walk through your neighborhood or around your yard. You will be more able to keep your mind open to new thoughts the Lord might introduce. You are likely to find yourself spending more time with Him.

13. "I have strayed like a lost sheep. Seek your servant, for I have not forgotten your commands" (Psalm 119:176).

Between you and the Lord, settle on a phrase that He can remind you of throughout the day to call you back into intimacy when you have turned your heart outward. Find a phrase like, "Only You." Use something short and simple that can be a "shorthand" prayer that speaks volumes.

14. "I thank my God every time I remember you" (Philippians 1:3).

This week, practice using "prayer triggers." Let even fleeting thoughts of your friends, loved ones, and "enemies" turn into prayer for them. The prayer can be as simple as breathing the name, "Jesus."

15. "I will sing to the LORD, for he has been good to me" (Psalm 13:6).

This week, during your prayer time, sing to the Lord. Use a hymnal or songbook; sing songs you have memorized; sing the Scriptures to your own tunes; make up songs. Sing aloud or sing inwardly.

16. "I spread out my hands to you; my soul thirsts for you like a parched land" (Psalm 143:6).

This week, during your prayer time, use different worship postures: kneel, lift your hands, fall on your face before Him. You may do this outwardly, or inwardly—in the inner sanctuary of your own soul.

17. "Praise be to the LORD, to God our Savior, who daily bears our burdens" (Psalm 68:19).

In your prayer journal, list the following headings: (1) Anxieties, (2) Responsibilities, (3) Needs, (4) Desires. Under each, list everything that comes to mind. As you write it down, consider it an act of surrender. You are handing each thing over to Him. Do this every day for a week. You will most likely be repeating some things every day. That's fine. He "*daily* bears our burdens."

18. "Here I am! I stand at the door and knock. If anyone hears my voice and opens the door, I will come in and eat with him, and he with me" (Revelation 3:20).

Prayer is opening your life to Jesus. He is at the door, knocking. In prayer, you are simply responding to His love that seeks you out. Times of prayer are times of fellowship with Him, as if He were in your home sharing a meal with you. This week, during your prayer time, let your mind's eye see Him as He sits just across from you. Talk right to Him and let Him talk to you.

19. "But seek his kingdom, and these things will be given to you as well" (Luke 12:31).

Your daily prayer time lays the groundwork for an ongoing awareness of His presence. This week, during your prayer time, ask Him to alert you and call your attention to "kingdom moments" throughout your day. Watch for opportunities to enjoy fellowship with Him—waiting in lines, performing mundane tasks, for example. Being consciously aware of His presence will transform life's irritants into opportunities for fellowship with Him.

20. "'Speak, for your servant is listening'" (1 Samuel 3:10*b*).

The most important prayer-skill is learning to listen to the Living Voice. This week, let listening to Him be the main focus of your prayer time. Let 1 Samuel 3:10 be your only request. Listen for Him in His Word, in the quietness of your heart, in the circumstances of your day, in fresh ideas that come to mind, in new understanding that settles on you. Learn to listen. Write down what you think you sense Him saying to you.

21. "Do not be anxious about anything, but in everything, by prayer and petition, with thanksgiving, present your requests to God. And the peace of God, which transcends all understanding, will guard your hearts and your minds in Christ Jesus" (Philippians 4:6–7).

What situations are causing you anxiety? Write them down. Big and little. Major and minor. Now, go back through your list and practice offering the sacrifice of thanksgiving as an act of obedience. First, thank God for allowing the circumstance in your life because you trust Him to bring about a good and beneficial outcome. Then, let the Spirit bring to your mind things that you can be thankful about in that circumstance—ways that you already see God's hand.

22. "Don't you know that you yourselves are God's temple and that God's Spirit lives in you?" (1 Corinthians 3:16).

You are God's dwelling place. He is at home in you. Focus on that reality this morning. You do not have to seek Him out and get His attention—He has sought you out. In the Old Testament, worship in the temple engaged all the senses. This week, create an atmosphere for your prayer time that engages your senses. Light a fragrant candle. Play worshipful music. Let your senses enter into the experience of worship.

23. "He wakens me morning by morning, wakens my ear to listen like one being taught" (Isaiah 50:4*a*).

This week, during your prayer time, consider that you are there at His invitation. He has invited you to spend time alone with Him because He has something beneficial to teach you and say to you. Consider how that changes the atmosphere of your prayer time. Write your observations in your journal.

24. "As a bridegroom rejoices over his bride, so will your God rejoice over you" (Isaiah 62:5*b*).

This week, begin your prayer time by feeling the Lord's pleasure in your presence. Be aware of how delighted He is to have time alone with you. Let His love for you and His joy in you fill your soul with peace and contentment.

25. "Whoever obeys his command will come to no harm, and the wise heart will know the proper time and procedure" (Ecclesiastes 8:5).

During your prayer times this week, ask the Lord to tell you anything He wants you to do today—any action He wants you to take. Express your faith to Him that, when the time comes, you will know what to do and how to do it. Be alert every moment of your day for His command.

26. "O LORD, you have searched me and you know me" (Psalm 139:1).

Each morning this week, during your prayer time, use Psalm 139:1–6. Read it through slowly each morning, concentrating on each phrase. Focus on a different verse each morning, turning it into your personal prayer and allowing the Spirit of God to speak personally to you. Keep that verse in your thoughts all day long, praying it as situations arise.

27. "Be still, and know that I am God" (Psalm 46:10*a*).

This week during your prayer times, focus on being in the moment. Let these words wrap themselves around your heart: "Be still. Know that I am God." Let the power of His presence flood you, filling you with confidence, peace, and boldness. When He says, "I am God," what is He saying to you? Each morning, write down what it means to you that He is God.

28. "Search me, O God, and know my heart; test me and know my anxious thoughts. See if there is any offensive way in me, and lead me in the way everlasting" (Psalm 139:23–24).

This week, open your life to the Father so that He can clean out the clutter. Let Him bring to light anything that is keeping you from experiencing all that He has to offer. Don't resist Him. He wants your life to be filled with His abundance and wants to rid you of anything that dilutes His power in you. Write down what He brings to mind.

29. "This is the day the LORD has made; [I will] rejoice and be glad in it" (Psalm 118:24).

This week, let this be your first thought every morning: *This* is the day the Lord has appointed for you. He has given you *this* day. Embrace everything He brings into this day. When it brings difficulty or disappointment, think of your circumstance as a "faith lab." Every little joy or pleasure it brings is a gift from the Father. Start your prayer times this week by settling this in your mind: I will rejoice and be glad in *this* day.

30. "Let this be written for a future generation, that a people not yet created may praise the LORD" (Psalm 102:18).

This week during your prayer time, compose a letter to future generations. Write a paragraph or a sentence or a thought each day. What do you want to pass along to those who will come after you? What do you want to leave them as a spiritual legacy? This will help you focus on what God means to you and will stir up genuine praise and worship.

31. "Those who know your name will trust in you, for you, LORD, have never forsaken those who seek you" (Psalm 9:10).

Each morning this week, focus on a name for Christ. Think through what that name says to you in your present circumstance. What promise does His name hold? As you pray, let Him show you each need or desire in light of His name—who He is. Use these names: (1) Refiner's Fire, Malachi 3:3; (2) God With Us, Matthew 1:23; (3) The Light, John 1:9; (4) Bread of Life, John 6:35; (5) Good Shepherd, John 10:11; (6) Master and Lord, John 13:13 KJV; (7) Vine, John 15:5.

32. "I have set the LORD always before me. Because he is at my right hand, I will not be shaken. Therefore my heart is glad and my tongue rejoices; my body also will rest secure" (Psalm 16:8–9).

Let the peace in your innermost being spill over into your body. This week, during your prayer times, start each morning by consciously relaxing. Breathe in deeply then breathe out slowly. As you breathe out, let your inner peace fill your body. Feel your muscles relaxing. Enjoy the feeling of complete peace and restfulness. Let thoughts of Him flood your mind and permeate your body with peace.

33. "Our Father in heaven, hallowed be your name" (Matthew 6:9).

Begin to pray through the Lord's Prayer, letting each phrase take root in your heart and grow fruit. This week, focus each morning on Matthew 6:9. Consider His role as Father. What does that mean in the context of your needs and desires? Write out your thoughts in your prayer journal. How can His name be exalted and hallowed in the midst of your needs? Write out your thoughts.

34. "Your kingdom come, your will be done on earth as it is in heaven" (Matthew 6:10).

This week, focus each morning on Matthew 6:10. Bring each situation to the Lord and pray, "Let Your will be done in this in every detail. Let Your kingdom rule take effect in this in every detail." Bring every detail of your situations before Him, asking Him to take full charge.

35. "Give us today our daily bread" (Matthew 6:11).

This week, focus each morning on Matthew 6:11. Ask Him for His provision in every circumstance and every need the day presents. Rest in His willingness and His ability to meet every need as it arises.

36. "Forgive us our debts, as we also have forgiven our debtors" (Matthew 6:12).

This week, focus on Matthew 6:12. Let the Father lead you in identifying and forgiving those who have hurt or offended you. Let Him set you free from the burden of bitterness.

37. "And lead us not into temptation, but deliver us from the evil one" (Matthew 6:13).

This week, focus on Matthew 6:13. Daily, ask the Lord to lead you in paths that will help you avoid temptation. Listen to Him as He brings thoughts to your mind about how to avoid placing yourself in temptation's path. Obey.

38. "That your ways may be known on earth, your salvation among all nations" (Psalm 67:2).

This week, use your newspaper or news magazine as a prayer guide. Find a current situation that engages your interest. Avoid the tendency to pray your political agenda. Instead, pray that every aspect of the situation will be God's tool for bringing about the right outcome for the big picture. Pray for every Christian who might be involved or affected. Pray for every non-believer. Pray for every detail you read about, including the media who are reporting it and the leaders who are making decisions. Pray that it will all work together to bring glory to His name.

39. "Carry each other's burdens, and in this way you will fulfill the law of Christ" (Galatians 6:2).

This week, ask the Lord to place on your mind someone for whom you are to pray. It may be someone you know well, or it may be someone with whom you are only acquainted. It may even be someone you only know of. Write the name down. Be faithful in praying each time the name comes to your remembrance. Watch for the amazing ways the Lord will lead you in prayer and the ways He will give you glimpses of His work. Write them in your journal.

40. "I have learned the secret of being content in any and every situation" (Philippians 4:12).

In which areas of your life do you lack contentment? Write them down as they come to mind. Are you looking to some external circumstance or some other person for contentment? This week, focus your prayer time on asking the Lord to create in you a heart that rests contentedly in Him and His plans for you.

41. "I urge you, brothers, by our Lord Jesus Christ and by the love of the Spirit, to join me in my struggle by praying to God for me" (Romans 15:30).

This week, ask someone else to pray for you in your struggles. Let the Lord guide you to the right person. During your prayer times, when your struggle comes to mind, rest in the fact that someone else is carrying that burden for you this week.

42. "When you fast, do not look somber as the hypocrites do, for they disfigure their faces to show men they are fasting. I tell you the truth, they have received their reward in full. But when you fast, put oil on your head and wash your face, so that it will not be obvious to men that you are fasting, but only to your Father, who is unseen; and your Father, who sees what is done in secret, will reward you" (Matthew 6:16–18).

This week, plan to fast one meal per day. Replace that meal with concentrated time in the Word of God and prayer. Let any hunger you experience serve as a call to prayer. Ask the Lord to give you as intense a craving for Him as your body has for food. Record your experience in your prayer journal each morning.

43. "He blesses the home of the righteous" (Proverbs 3:33*b*).

This week, have your time of prayer in a different room in your home each morning. Focus your prayer time around the aspect of your life or your family's life that room represents to you. Let the Spirit bring ideas to mind.

44. "I will walk in my house with blameless heart" (Psalm 101:2*b*).

This week, focus your prayer time on your relationship with each member of your family, or those who are like family to you. Each morning, concentrate on one person. Pray for God's purpose to be established in that relationship. Ask Him to show you any ways that your heart is not blameless in your own home.

45. "The word is very near you; it is in your mouth and in your heart so you may obey it" (Deuteronomy 30:14).

This week, during your prayer times, read the Scripture aloud. You will find that your mind stays focused better and that hearing the words and speaking them brings out nuances that you have missed by reading silently.

46. "Therefore encourage one another and build each other up, just as in fact you are doing" (1 Thessalonians 5:11).

This week, prepare for your daily prayer time by gathering note cards or stationary of some sort. Ask the Lord to place on your heart someone who needs encouragement. During your prayer time, write out your prayer for that person and mail it to him or her. Pray for and encourage someone different each morning.

47. "We always thank God for all of you, mentioning you in our prayers. We continually remember before our God and Father your work produced by faith, your labor prompted by love, and your endurance inspired by hope in our Lord Jesus Christ" (1 Thessalonians 1:2–3).

This week, keep your stationary handy. During your prayer times, let the Spirit remind you of people who have been instrumental in your spiritual formation. As you are thanking God for them, write notes of appreciation to them. Some may be currently in your life. Some may be from years before. Rejoice in the treasure God has put in your life in the form of His people.

48. "Finally, be strong in the Lord and in his mighty power. Put on the full armor of God so that you can take your stand against the devil's schemes....And pray in the Spirit on all occasions with all kinds of prayers and requests. With this in mind, be alert and always keep on praying for all the saints" (Ephesians 6:10–11, 18).

This week, pray through the spiritual armor that Paul describes in Ephesians 6:10–18. Each morning, read the entire passage, expecting the Spirit to make it fresh for you. Then, each day focus on one piece of armor. Let the Lord speak to you about it as you spiritually "put it on." (1) Belt of Truth, (2) Breastplate of Righteousness, (3) Shoes of the Gospel of Peace, (4) Shield of Faith, (5) Helmet of Salvation, (6) Sword of the Spirit. On the seventh day, read verse 18 carefully. Once armed, how do you take your stand against the devil's schemes? Through prayer.

49. "Many are the plans in a man's heart, but it is the LORD's purpose that prevails" (Proverbs 19:21).

This week, focus your prayer time on embracing the Lord's purpose in your every action, every plan, and every endeavor. Each morning, list your plans for the day. Yield them to God's purposes. Be ready to change them if the Lord should direct you to. Be alert for how God is working out His long-term purposes through your short-term plans.

50. "Let us fix our eyes on Jesus, the author and perfecter of our faith" (Hebrews 12:2*a*).

This week, be fully aware of Jesus. He is God's Everything. During your daily prayer time, before you do anything else, fix your inner eyes on Jesus. As you go through your day, let your inner eyes see Jesus present in every situation. When you think of a friend or a family member, let your inner eyes see Jesus there with that person.

51. "I guide you in the way of wisdom and lead you along straight paths. When you walk, your steps will not be hampered; when you run, you will not stumble" (Proverbs 4:11–12).

This week, turn this promise into a prayer. Memorize these verses or write them out and take them with you. Pray this promise as you make every decision—big or little, business or personal. Record your experiences in your prayer journal.

52. "I pray also that the eyes of your heart may be enlightened in order that you may know the hope to which he has called you" (Ephesians 1:18).

This week, plan a prayer excursion. Go by yourself, enlist a fellow intercessor, or go as a prayer group. Go to a public place—a mall, a restaurant, a ball game. Pray "flash prayers" for people you encounter. Ask God to open the eyes of their hearts so that they will know the hope to which He has called them. If you are with a partner or a group, you may wish to pray aloud in conversational tones. You do not need to close your eyes to pray.

also by Jennifer Kennedy Dean

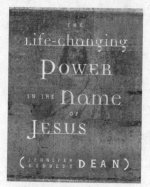

The Life-Changing Power in the Name of Jesus

Learn how to live in the power of the name above all names.
1-56309-841-5

The Life-Changing Power in the Blood of Christ

Explores the immense power of the blood of Christ in the life of the believer.
1-56309-753-2

Riches Stored in Secret Places: A Devotional Guide for Those Who Hunger After God

For every believer who longs to pursue the secret mysteries of God's Word.
1-56309-203-4

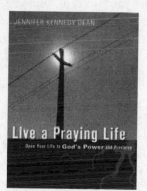

Live a Praying Life: Open Your Life to God's Power and Provision

Tackles the complex question: If God is sovereign, why pray?
1-56309-752-4

Legacy of Prayer: A Spiritual Trust Fund for the Generations

Illustrates that God has initiated a covenant with believers to cover their children, and prayer is the conduit that brings the power of that covenant into the circumstances of earth.
1-56309-711-7

Available in Christian bookstores everywhere

new hope
PUBLISHERS

Inspiring Women. Changing Lives.

To schedule

Jennifer Kennedy Dean

for your next event, please contact

The Praying Life Foundation
Post Office Box 62
Blue Springs, MO 64013
888.844.6647
seminars@prayinglife.org

Visit **www.prayinglife.org** to:

- Find answers to frequently asked questions
- Ask Jennifer your own questions
- Find a monthly column by Jennifer
- Discover a wealth of resources for your praying life

new
hope
PUBLISHERS

Inspiring Women. Changing Lives.